LEON METCALFE

D1033635

Discovering
Ghosts

SHIRE PUBLICATIONS LTD

ACKNOWLEDGEMENTS
The cover design is by Felix Partridge. Photographs are acknowledged as
follows: Ashmolean Museum, page 68; George W. F. Ellis, page 63; Robin
Laurance, page 41; Leon Metcalfe, pages 11, 16, 25, 29, 33, 36, 37, 42, 51,
52, 55, 67, 69, 81 and 82; Patrick Wise, page 64; Geoffrey N. Wright, page
73. All other photographs are by Cadbury Lamb.

British Library Cataloguing in Publication Data: Metcalfe, Leon.
Discovering Ghosts. – 2 Rev.ed. – (Discovering Series; No. 147). I. Title.
II. Series. 398.470941. ISBN 0-7478-0164-9.

08/2/2

*Published in 2008 by Shire Publications Ltd, Midland House, West Way,
Botley, Oxfordshire OX2 0PH.*
*Copyright © 1972 and 1994 by Leon Metcalfe. First published 1972,
reprinted 1974, 1979, 1983 and 1987; second edition, extended with new
material, 1994; reprinted 2008. Number 147 in the Discovering series.
ISBN 978 0 7478 0164 1.*

Printed in Great Britain by Ashford Colour Press Ltd, Unit 600, Fareham
Reach, Fareham Road, Gosport, Hampshire PO16 0FW.

CONTENTS

1
GHOSTS OF MURDERERS AND THEIR VICTIMS

The Cunliffes of Wycoller Hall

To the east of the busy Lancashire town of Colne, a turning right off the A6068 through Winewall eventually leads to Wycoller, a village hidden in a secret valley. The lane descends and twists and turns, criss-crossing the beck as though reluctant to allow visitors into this apparent haven of peace. The car may be parked at the far end of the village, beyond the Craft Centre.

Across the first of Wycoller's famous bridges, a double-arched packhorse bridge, the roofless but menacingly forbidding old hall comes into view. This is all that remains of what was once the largest residence in the village. It was built towards the end of the sixteenth century by the Hartley family and survived into the twentieth century after being improved and extended in 1774 and 1775. This work was undertaken by Henry Owen Cunliffe, who hoped thereby to attract a wealthy wife rather than to marry some local lady. He succeeded in his aim but his lifestyle was so extravagant that he was still heavily mortgaged when he died.

The ghostly goings on at **Wycoller** are not the doings of Henry but of a Cunliffe of the Stuart period some 150 years earlier. The most popular version tells of the action taking place just once a year, and then only when the wind is howling along the valley and ripping through the tree tops, causing them to grind and crack, while stinging torrential rain is swept along by the tempest. Above the sounds of the raging storm is heard the clattering of hooves, as a lone rider, dressed in a hood and full-length cape, gallops his horse through the village, across the packhorse bridge and up to the front porch of the hall. Dismounting almost before his horse stops, he rushes through the doorway. From here he ascends the broad staircase at a run and enters a bedroom. The sounds emanating from this room are those of a woman being very badly treated and, as her screams weaken into low moans, the phantom rider reappears at the front door, leaps on his agitated steed and gallops off into the stormy night.

The rider is reputed to be a Cunliffe who, having discovered his wife had a lover, murdered her in the violent fashion which is re-enacted in the haunting.

The episode, however, is not necessarily completed there, for they do say that the Lady in Black, at other times called Black Bess or Old Bess, is the troubled spectre of the murdered lady. She does not seem to bear a grudge against those who see her nowadays and she shows no malice when she has been observed in the grounds by people visiting the ruins. Her only response to an approach or challenge is to disappear quietly. They say that as she was dying, she cursed the Cunliffes and swore to see the end of their line. As will be appreciated, this took a long time to achieve and perhaps she lingers out of habit or to ensure that the family does not attempt a return.

An intriguing alternative to the Black Bess story reports that one of the Cunliffes, who had travelled to the New World to make his fortune, had married a coloured bride in the West Indies. Whilst sailing home to receive his inheritance and to become master of Wycoller Hall, he is said to have had misgivings and regrets about his marriage and solved the problem by tipping his wife overboard to drown her.

The double-arched packhorse bridge and the simple clapper bridge at Wycoller, Lancashire.

The body may have drowned but the spirit of Black Bess lingered on and followed her errant husband back to his family seat, where she gave him no peace and continues to visit the area from time to time.

The lady highwayman

On the A5 in Hertfordshire, five miles from Luton, is the village of **Markyate**. To the north of the church lies Markyate Cell, a neo-Elizabethan mansion which incorporates parts of the original dwelling, the Cell. This was a hermitage built in the early part of the twelfth century by Roger, a monk of St Albans. During the sixteenth century Humphrey Bouchier obtained the land and a new house was built.

When Humphrey died his widow married George Ferrers, and one of their descendants in the seventeenth century was Katherine Ferrers. She had the misfortune to be married off at the age of thirteen to a boy of sixteen with whom she could never form a happy and successful partnership. This, it is thought, prompted her to lead a somewhat unusual life for a lady of her position.

About the year 1645 Lady Katherine assumed the role of a highwayman, terrorising the travellers on Watling Street by holding them up at gunpoint as she sat astride her huge black horse, or by swinging out on to the road from overhanging trees. She robbed and killed as the fancy took her, but for a long time she managed to keep her second identity a secret. In order to do this she had constructed in the mansion a secret staircase starting on the ground floor beside the chimney and leading up to a small chamber on the floor above where she stored her highwayman's disguise.

Eventually a guard on a coach she was trying to rob managed to get a shot at her. She was mortally wounded and, although she had life enough in her to escape from the scene of the shooting, she died at the entrance to her secret room. Her body was found, still dressed in highwayman's garb, and the secret was out.

Efforts were made to hush the affair up. Her 'private apartment' was immediately bricked up, but all to no avail, for the story swept round the locality. It was not long before the people of the area began to see her ghost re-enacting many of her former criminal activities, complete with her phantom horse.

The secret room of Lady Ferrers was 'lost' after a fire destroyed much of the house in 1841 and during subsequent rebuilding.

The farmer with a hole in his chest

A mile and a half from the centre of **Thame**, Oxfordshire, along the A418 towards Aylesbury is a right turn leading to the village of **Haddenham**. It is at this junction that you may see the ghost of a

The A418 Thame to Aylesbury road at its junction with the road to Haddenham, Buckinghamshire.

man staggering along clutching at a gaping, bleeding hole in his chest. Having seen this apparition, take care, for this is his way of warning of impending danger.

The man died late one evening in 1828 as he was returning from Thame market to his farm, where his wife was waiting for him. As it was very late and he had not returned, she went to the farmhouse door and looked out into the night for him. She saw him, but not as she expected, for his ghost slowly materialised before her eyes holding his wounded chest from which protruded the shaft of a heavy hammer. The distraught woman rushed out for help, and the body of her husband was found by the roadside with wounds corresponding to those seen on the ghost.

An immediate investigation was carried out into the murder, but no arrests were made. Many people thought at the time that the farmer's wife was guilty, since she was the first to raise the alarm and knew the cause of death even before the body was discovered. Later, however, it was discovered that the farmer had seen two men, Tylor and Sewell, stealing sheep and threatened to report their crime, which in those days was punishable with transportation. The two men had murdered him to silence him for ever. Both were tried and convicted and they were publicly hanged on 8th March 1830 outside Aylesbury Prison.

The murderous monk

To reach the haunted **Lidwell Chapel** in Devon leave Dawlish westward along Weech Road to the T junction. Turn left towards Luscombe Hill and Haldon. Continue straight on along Aller Road past the turning on the right to Dawlish Water and Haldon. Drive up the lane under the bridge and keep to the main track, which is almost two miles long and passes Southwood Farm on its way to Lidwell Farm. These are the only two inhabited dwellings along the length of this lane.

The chapel lies on private farmland, so seek permission from the farmer at Lidwell Farm before continuing your journey on foot. No doubt the farmer will indicate the general route to the chapel and direct you to the left of his barn beside the stream. Follow the track across the meadow to the gate on your right. Through the gate keep to the right of the field and proceed uphill to the bulge in the hedge where the remains of the chapel are clothed in trees and brambles.

The end wall of the chapel is the most complete part of this sadly neglected ruin. Having approached so close through the tangle of undergrowth it is a little incongruous to find that the ruin is protected by a neat, well-painted, green iron railing. The entrance gate is at the far end of the chapel. Unfortunately the well which figures in this ghost story cannot now be traced; even the farmer does not know its location.

Our story centres on a sailor who, after many years at sea, decided to retire and, with the pack on his back full of booty, made his way from the coast inland. Towards evening, as he neared Lidwell Chapel, a great storm blew up. When he reached the chapel he was invited in by the monk in residence there, to shelter from the storm. The sailor gratefully accepted the offer and entered, removing his pack and soaked outer garments.

As the evening wore on the monk listened to the many tales which the sailor had to tell. Eventually the monk began to show displeasure at some of the sailor's former activities and asked him if he had been baptised. The sailor admitted that he had not, and so the monk offered to baptise him at the start of his new life ashore. The sailor accepted and was led over to a font in a dark corner of the chapel where he knelt down. Suddenly a feeling of fear and suspicion swept over the sailor and he wheeled round to see the monk standing above him with a dagger poised. The two wrestled and the sailor overcame the evil monk. To keep him secure until the matter was reported to the authorities, the sailor put him down the well and set off for the nearest village.

Later that night the sailor and a party of villagers returned to the chapel and hauled the monk from his temporary prison. They found him in an excessive state of fear and panic, clawing at the well shaft in an effort to extricate himself. On investigating the bottom of the well they found it to be littered with the remains of earlier travellers who had passed that way and been less fortunate than the sailor.

The ghost of the monk has been seen and heard, his head and shoulders out of the top of the well, struggling vigorously to escape from his victims and his murderous past.

Wicked Will and the midwife

Littlecote House in Wiltshire, which is now a hotel, two miles north west of Hungerford on the A4192, came into the possession of the Darrell family in 1415, though the present Tudor manor-house was built between 1490 and 1520. The last of the Darrells of Littlecote was Will, nicknamed Wild or Wicked Will. The aptness of these nicknames this story will reveal.

Will Darrell had many mistresses, including his own sister, and one of them became pregnant by him. When she was close to giving birth, Darrell sent two servants to bring back, with the promise of great reward, a well-known local midwife, Mother Barnes. For her part she had to agree to the utmost secrecy, which included bringing her to the house blindfolded. On arriving at Mother Barnes's house in Great Shefford the men explained their errand in only the briefest detail, so that she did not know where she was going and had no idea of the identity of the persons involved. She agreed, however, and rode pillion behind one of the two messengers.

At Littlecote she was hurried upstairs to the bedroom where the woman lay in labour, and her blindfold was removed. Throughout the night she carried out her duties until the child, a boy, was born. Nothing had been prepared in which to dress the child, so Mother Barnes wrapped him in her large white apron and carried him out on to the landing, where Wild Will Darrell was warming himself in front of the fire. Will took the child from Mother Barnes and thrust

Littlecote House, Wiltshire, house of Wild Will Darrell.

him on the fire, holding him with his boot in position among the flames until he was no more.

When night came Mother Barnes was taken back to her house, blindfolded once again. She had, however, endeavoured to gather what little evidence she could relating to the house she was in by snipping from the bed curtains a section of material and, on leaving, by counting the number of stairs from the landing to the ground floor.

Later, when the whole terrible tale had been told, Wild Will was arrested. The evidence against him was strong, for Mother Barnes's information and exhibits matched exactly the number of stairs at Littlecote and the missing piece from the bed curtains. By the time of the trial, however, Mother Barnes was dead and she could not, therefore, identify Darrell as the murderer, and so he was found not guilty and released. He was later killed in a riding accident when his horse reared up on seeing the ghost of the baby and threw Will, who broke his neck. This occurred in the park at a place still known as 'Darrell's Stile'.

It is interesting to note that after the death of Will Darrell in 1589 the new owner of the house was Sir John Popham, the judge at Will's trial!

The whole awful scene is re-enacted by the ghosts of those involved in what is known in the house as the Haunted Landing and the Haunted Bedroom.

The girl starved by her governess

There are several ghosts which haunt **Herstmonceux Castle**, East Sussex. East of Hailsham on the A271, at Herstmonceux village turn down Chapel Row, which leads on to Church Road and then up to the gates of Herstmonceux Castle on the left. The moated brick castle was begun in 1440 by Sir Roger de Fiennes and its main feature is the massive gatehouse. It was largely dismantled in 1777 and remained in a ruinous state until restored in 1933.

The most recent ghost is that of a young woman who died on the eve of her 21st birthday in 1727. She was due to inherit vast wealth when she was 21 but her cruel governess received payments from a person who would benefit from the girl's death for disposing of her before she reached the age of majority. The governess did this by slowly starving her to death. The poor, emaciated girl is seen wandering beside the moat.

The phantom drummer of Herstmonceux

Up on the castle ramparts may be seen the towering nine foot tall figure of a drummer beating out a rhythmical tattoo. This ghost is of uncertain origin; some say he died at the battle of Agincourt while in the service of Sir Roger de Fiennes, builder of the castle, others that he is the ghost of a man who suddenly and unaccountably decided to become a hermit while living in the castle. His wife was young and beautiful and, after her husband had shut himself away, many suitors sought her hand, thinking that she was a widow. Each one, however, was frightened away by the hermit beating his drum and pretending to haunt the castle. The wife became so infuriated with her husband that one day she locked him in his room and refused to let him out, so that he died a prolonged death from starvation. However, he had the last laugh on his wife by continuing his fearful drumming long after his death!

The smuggler with the severed head

Happisburgh is a village on the Norfolk coast between Cromer and Great Yarmouth, situated on the B1159. From the church, take a left turning, and it is only a short walk to the cliffs and the coast. To the south and a little way inland can be seen a red and white

Happisburgh lighthouse, Norfolk, is on the route of the ghostly smuggler.

painted lighthouse, which was built in 1791 by the Trinity House Brethren. It is a pleasant walk along the cliffs, overlooking the sea and a sandy beach, to Cart Gap. It is from here, across to the lighthouse and up the village street of Happisburgh that a ghost passes.

He is seen on moonlit nights traversing this route, though legless and apparently headless, yet clutching firmly a bundle in his arms. He was first seen in the early 1800s by local people who thought that he was headless as he came towards them. In profile, however, it was seen that the peculiar hump on his back was his almost severed head drooping down behind him! Carefully he was followed until eventually he disappeared down into the depths of a village well.

The following morning the observers recounted the event to the village council and it was decided to try to substantiate their story by investigating the well. A man with a grappling hook was lowered into the well on a sling. At the bottom he ranged about with his hook until contact was made with an object. He signalled to the men above, who hauled him and his 'catch' to the surface. The man had brought up with him a sack similar to the one the ghost had been clutching and when it was opened a pair of boots was revealed. Still in the boots were the legs of the unfortunate ghost! The dredging of the well continued, and the torso and hanging head were brought up. Round the body was a belt and still tucked into the belt was a pistol. The well revealed no more but, retracing the track taken by the ghost, the investigators discovered near Cart Gap a pistol matching the one on the body, gold pieces, bloodstains and broken bottles, all the signs of a fierce struggle.

With all the evidence assembled, it was thought that the ghost was a smuggler who had met his gory death through disagreeing with his associates over the division of their booty. No one, however, has been brought to justice over this crime, and the ghost seems doomed to his roaming for ever.

The woman who warned of the Gunpowder Plot

A couple of miles off the A227, north of Tonbridge in Kent, is **Ightham Mote,** a moated manor-house built in 1340 and changed little outwardly since that date. From the time of Elizabeth I to the middle of the reign of Victoria, Ightham Mote was the home of only one family, the Selbys, who were devout Catholics. Consequently the house has its secret escape route and secret hiding places.

To be aware of the ghost of Ightham you must be sensitive to variations in temperature, for this is the only sense which will

At Ightham Mote in Kent the ghost chills the air.

initially be aroused when the ghost is at hand. In the tower people were aware of a sudden chillness in the air but no explanation could be found for it until, towards the end of the nineteenth century, workmen discovered a fourteenth-century window and a blocked-up doorway, together indicating a secret room. This was broken into and within was discovered the skeleton of a woman.

It is thought that this must be the skeleton of Dorothy Selby, who is believed to have sent the anonymous letter to Lord Monteagle warning him not to attend the Houses of Parliament on 5th November 1605. She was thereby instrumental in causing the failure of the Gunpowder Plot. According to the story she was imprisoned in her little room by persons sympathetic to the cause of the conspirators.

The Green Lady

The village of **Swanbourne** in Buckinghamshire stands on slightly elevated land on the B4032 between Winslow and Leighton Buzzard. The church of St Swithin dominates the village and Manor Farm, a stone-built house in the form of a cross, dating from 1632, stands beside the church. Across the road from the church lies another stone-built dwelling, the Tudor manor-house. Now a retirement home, it was once the seat of the Cottesloe family. There are several other interesting houses in the village but our attention is concentrated on the area described, as this is the haunt of Swanbourne's 'Green Lady'. Little is known about her but one theory is that she is Elizabeth Adams, wife of Thomas Adams. A memorial brass depicting husband, wife and their four children can be seen in the floor of the church. Included on the brass is an inscription relating the death of Thomas in October 1627 as follows:

> Behold in him the fickle state of man
> Which holie David likened to a span
> Who in prime of youth by bloudy theves was slaine
> In Liscombe ground his blood ye grasse did staine.

Elizabeth died heartbroken soon after the murder of her husband, but she found no peace in death for, as the 'Green Lady', dressed as depicted on the brass, she haunts the village in her distress searching perhaps for the 'bloudy theves' who murdered her Thomas.

A favourite and a favourite's wife

Scarborough Castle in North Yorkshire has a long and fascinating history dating from the time of the Romans. The ghost, however, dates only from the reign of Edward II when Piers Gaveston, Earl of Cornwall and the king's favourite, was captured there and executed. Since then he has constantly sought revenge on the living by lurking in deep shadows cast by the gaunt castle walls, and by luring innocent people to the cliff edge and beyond to their deaths.

Scarborough Castle, North Yorkshire.

A sadder phantom haunts the village of **Cumnor**, situated off the A420 south-west of Oxford. Cumnor Hall, which once stood south-west of the church, was the home of Amy Robsart in the time of Elizabeth I. Her husband was Robert Dudley, Earl of Leicester, one of the queen's favourites. It was rumoured that he arranged Amy's 'accidental' fall down the main staircase of the hall, thus causing her death and the subsequent haunting.

The drunken drummer's phantom hearse

The Devil himself, escorted by a huge black hound, in a great storm visited **Blythburgh**, a village on the A12 in east Suffolk, on Sunday 4th August 1577. He descended on the church, destroying the steeple and bringing down the great bell, killing members of the congregation and leaving others stricken and grovelling. Scorch marks can still be seen today where the Devil made his exit through the north door!

But Blythburgh has a more normal haunting, the story of which began at the White Hart inn across the road from the church. During June 1750 a regiment of dragoons was billeted in the village and among them was a black drummer called Tobias Gill. Toby, as he was called, was a drunkard and one night he became so drunk that the landlord of the White Hart, refusing to serve him any more, turned him out into the night. He must have staggered the length of the village to the heath. There he came upon Ann Blakemore, a girl from Walberswick. He grabbed her and she fought to escape, but in vain, for he raped and then strangled her. His exertions sapped the last of his energy and he was found the next morning asleep by the cold lifeless body of his victim.

He was tried, found guilty and hanged on 14th September 1750 near the place where the murder was committed. As was the custom his body was left to hang for a long time as a warning to others of the penalty to be paid for such a crime.

Toby's Walks, as the area to the south-west of the village is called, is the place to visit in order to see Toby's own ghostly version of the funeral procession never offered to him. The hearse, pulled by four black horses, hurtles across the heath at breakneck speed with Black Toby at the reins excitedly urging more speed from his phantom chargers.

Some other murderers' ghosts

The abbey ruins at **Bury St Edmunds**, Suffolk, house the ghosts of many monks and of a nun, Maude Carew. She haunts those fascinating houses which are built into the ruined west front of the abbey church. It is there that Maude is reputed to have poisoned Humphrey, Duke of Gloucester, during his imprisonment in 1446.

Houses built into the ruined abbey at Bury St Edmunds, Suffolk.

She appears as the Grey Lady, passing through rooms and people.

In the fellows' garden of Christ's College, **Cambridge**, is a mulberry tree planted by John Milton and haunted by Christopher Round clad in black and still paying penance for murdering a fellow of the college.

The area round **Brede Place**, north of Hastings, East Sussex, is haunted by the ghost of Sir Goddard, a giant of a man and a baby-eater who was dragged off to Groaning Bridge and sawn in half by angry villagers when his crimes were discovered. No wonder he is still haunting the district!

Victims of brutal crimes

If you should have to travel the A329 in Berkshire between **Bracknell** and **Ascot** at night do not be surprised if you are confronted by a policeman on foot without a police car in sight. The policeman, with his badly mutilated face, is the ghost of a pre-mechanised bobby who must have been horribly murdered while doing his duty.

Great Leighs, off the A131 Roman road south of Braintree, Essex, claims to have the 'oldest inn in England', the St Anne's Castle inn. This contains a haunted room where many people have attempted to pass the night but have always been disturbed by knocks, thuds, scrapings, cold draughts and clammy feelings. Even the bed clothes have been ripped from their bodies! Black shapes have been seen and cries like those of a child have been heard. Tradition has it that a child was murdered in the room before the eyes of its distraught mother.

Off the A274, west of Ashford, Kent, is **Smarden** and the fourteenth-century inn called the Chequers. In the oldest part of the inn a passage connecting two bedrooms is haunted by a soldier who was murdered there by the locals. The reason for this murder is not known, but you will recognise him if you see him for he is dressed in soldier's uniform of the Napoleonic Wars.

A monk who speaks Elizabethan English and who was killed in the reign of Henry VIII haunts **Westminster Abbey**. The most popular time and place to see him is between 5 and 6 p.m. in the abbey cloisters. The legend is that he was killed by thieves who stabbed him to death while robbing the abbey of its treasures.

The victim of another London murder was the actor William Terriss. He was stabbed to death as he left the Adelphi theatre in December 1897, and his ghost now haunts the theatre, **Covent Garden** tube station and the surrounding area.

The sixteenth-century Bull Hotel at **Long Melford**, a village in Suffolk north of Sudbury off the A134, has experienced within its walls many activities which can only be attributed to a poltergeist. Much crockery, heavy copper jugs and pewter coffee pots have been moved or hurled about the rooms, while fires have been started without human aid. There is no known reason for these phenomena except that in 1648 a Richard Everard was murdered in

Covent Garden tube station, London, is haunted by an actor.

the entrance hall by a man named Richard Greene.

Seven miles south-east of Rhyl in North Wales is the small village of **Cwm**, where the Blue Lion inn is haunted by a farm labourer named John Henry, who was murdered there in 1646. John Henry's ghost is rarely seen but his footsteps have been heard pacing the floors of the old inn.

2
TROUBLED
SPIRITS

The monk who fell asleep

A mile and a half south of Wisbech, Cambridgeshire, on the A1101 is a turning on the right to **Elm**. The church is on the left about half a mile down this road. The vicarage is built on the site of an old monastery where, more than 750 years ago, there lived a monk by the name of Ignatius. Ignatius, the spirit, has made at least one good friend amongst the modern living. This was the wife of a rector of Elm, who conversed quite freely with the ancient ghost and thereby learned much of his sad story.

Ignatius was not an evil man during his lifetime. He has, however, been suffering these past seven centuries for a careless lapse in his daily routine. One of the monk's jobs in the monastery, which was located in the low-lying land a few miles south of the Wash, was to keep careful watch for approaching flood waters, which could so easily engulf the monastery. On this fateful occasion poor Ignatius succumbed to his drowsiness and fell asleep on watch. The flood water came rushing across the land towards the monastery and no alarm bell was rung. Several monks were drowned in their cells and Ignatius has been paying for their deaths ever since.

Nowadays when 'the bell of Ignatius' is heard, it is supposed to signify not the coming of a flood but a death in the parish.

The blotted copy-book

A mile or so beyond the famous suspension bridge over the Thames from Marlow is the village of **Bisham** in Berkshire. On the right is Bisham Abbey, a Tudor house now owned by the Central Council of Physical Recreation. The present owners and the athletes who make use of the excellent facilities at the Abbey have the Elizabethan Lady Hoby to contend with!

Elizabeth Hoby was an educated woman, well versed in Greek and Latin and apparently not a little intolerant of the educational inadequacies of others; for the story goes that her young son William was constantly chastised for the poor work he produced during his lessons. Lady Hoby finally became so infuriated with his untidy blot-ridden books that she either scolded him and locked him away in an airless room or, in another version, beat him so

Bisham Abbey, Berkshire, where Lady Hoby laments the death of her son.

unmercifully that he died.

With the weight of her son's death hanging heavy on her heart, it was not long before Lady Elizabeth also died. However, her death did not bring peace and tranquillity to her soul, for soon afterwards she reappeared as a sorrowing woman, pacing the corridors and washing her son's blood from her hands in an apparently unsupported bowl which floated ahead of her. Her ghost has been frequently reported haunting Bisham Abbey throughout the centuries.

Some confirmation of this story was unearthed in the 1850s when workmen found a secret cache of children's copy-books, some bearing the name William Hoby, and they were covered with blots! Unfortunately this evidence has been lost.

The rector who broke his word

Vernham Dean, a lonely village in the centre of a delightfully rural area of Hampshire framed by the A338, A342 and A343, was unfortunate enough in 1665 to be affected by the plague. The rector at that time persuaded the sufferers to leave the village and ascend the hill to the ancient Fosbury Camp, where he promised to supply them with food and drink. It was hoped that by doing this the plague would be confined and controlled. It was, but the rector did not fulfil his part of the bargain and the suffering villagers died of plague and starvation in the ancient camp. Since then the penitent ghost of the rector has been doomed to mount the hill from the village, weighed down by remorse and the provisions he failed to carry during his lifetime.

Another repentant ghost is a phantom horseman, one of the knights who murdered Thomas à Becket in Canterbury Cathedral on 29th December 1170. On the anniversary of his crime he rides up to the church at **Kemsing**, north of Sevenoaks and the M26 in Kent, dismounts, and having entered kneels in prayer.

The woodcutter's girl

On 17th March every year crowds of people assemble at the Ferry Boat Inn in **Holywell** near St Ives in Cambridgeshire, for on that night the ghost of Juliet Tousley appears, so it is said, as it has done for centuries. Juliet was in love with Tom Zoul, a woodcutter, but her feelings were not reciprocated. They quarrelled and Juliet went and hanged herself from a willow beside the Ouse, clad in her best pink dress. She was buried beside the river beneath a stone slab. The Ferry Boat Inn was subsequently built over the spot, and the slab can be seen in its floor. Juliet Tousley soon regretted her hasty suicide and each year on the anniversary of her death her ghost returns to the scene of her death and burial by the Ouse.

On 17th March each year Juliet Tousley returns to the Ferry Boat Inn, Holywell, Cambridgeshire.

3
DOMESTIC DISASTERS

The Lady in White and her cruel husband

From the crossroads in **Skipsea** in the East Riding of Yorkshire take the B1249 Beeford road. Beyond the church is a notice 'Skipsea Brough – ancient monument', which points the way to the entrance to the castle mound. Nothing remains standing on the castle mound except, on occasions, the Lady in White. She is the ghost who has haunted the castle area for eight hundred years or more. Please help her if you see her, for she is searching for someone to help her recover her body, which is buried somewhere about.

Her story begins in Norman England for she was the niece of William the Conqueror and had the misfortune to marry Droge de Bevere, a Norman knight who had been given these lands by the Conqueror for his help during the invasion. Droge was insanely cruel, not only to his wife, but also to his children and his serfs. Only his wife remained faithful and loyal to him, but eventually she too suffered the ultimate in cruelty from him. He poisoned her and buried the body to hide his evil deed.

He then requested permission from William to journey abroad with his wife, in order that he might show her the place of her birth. Naturally William agreed to the request and this gave Droge the time and opportunity to make good his escape before William discovered the murder of his niece. Everything worked to plan and Droge was out of reach even of William when the murder came to light.

Lady de Bevere may be seen at any time of day or night and she may be headed or headless. The poison she drank must have been powerful stuff!

The girl who loved her home

The early seventeenth-century **Burton Agnes Hall** lies midway between Driffield and Bridlington, in the East Riding of Yorkshire, set back off the A614. In the grounds of this beautiful old house is the original Norman hall dating from 1173.

Sir Henry Griffith, the builder of Burton Agnes Hall, had three daughters. There is a portrait on view in the hall showing all three, the youngest of whom was Anne. Anne was a kind, sensitive girl who had been delighted with the building of their new home. She eagerly awaited its completion as she loved the place so dearly. It had not been finished long when Anne took a walk with her dog across the countryside to visit the St Quentins of Harpham Hall, a mile away. No doubt she discussed with her friends there the joys of living in the new house.

In the evening she began her journey home, meeting on the way some itinerant mendicants, or wold rangers as they were called in those parts, who asked for alms. As she took off her glove to open her purse she revealed a valuable ring on her finger. Seeing this, the rangers clubbed and robbed her. She was found unconscious later that night and carried back to the hall.

Before she died, five days later, she begged her sisters to preserve her skull and to keep it in the hall which she loved so much. To humour her in her last hours they agreed to her request, but when she died her complete remains were buried in Burton Agnes church.

There followed a very noisy and disturbed period for the inhabitants of the hall: there were crashes and groans and the loud slamming of doors. The vicar, Sir William St Quentin, was asked for his advice and he suggested that Anne be exhumed and her skull placed in the hall as she had requested. The advice was accepted and the body was exhumed. When the coffin lid was raised the body appeared intact but it was surmounted by a grin-

Burton Agnes Hall, Humberside.

ning skull. The skull was carried reverently into the hall and peace came to Burton Agnes.

Only on two occasions has this peace been shattered. The first was when a cleaning girl threw the skull out of the window and it landed on a horse-drawn manure cart. The horse refused to budge an inch until the skull had been removed and replaced in the hall. The second occasion was when the Boynton family owned the hall and the skull was taken out into the garden and buried. The original noises and groans recommenced, to cease only when the skull was brought inside again.

The last that was heard of the skull was that it had been bricked up in the walls of the hall so that there would be no chance of it straying again. No record of where the skull rests was kept but, wherever it is, the spirit of Anne Griffith remains quiet and peaceful.

The son who was killed in India

A mile from Wallingford, Oxfordshire, along the A4130 Henley road, across the Thames, is a right turn for Ipsden. Three miles along this country lane, away to the right is a spinney which hides **Ipsden** church, inside which is an organ-loft screen erected in memory of John and Ann Marie Reade, who lived in Ipsden House.

Opposite the church is a cart track which leads to the village. On arriving at the village road turn right and walk to the large tree on the small triangular green at the junction of three roads. Up the lane on the left is Ipsden House, home of the Reade family. There was once a donkey-wheel well there.

Take the lane beside the barn set on staddlestones and look out for a large horse-chestnut tree 200 yards away in the field to the left of the road. On the right as you approach this tree is a green road, part of the Icknield Way. Opposite this there is a gap in the hedge affording access to the chestnut tree. Walk round the thicket and tree until there on the right, overgrown through neglect, is a monument surrounded by low railings. It is of white stone rising to a pyramid and bearing the inscription:

John Thurlow Reade
Esquire
Sehaarunpore
November 25 A.D. 1827
'Alas my brother'

This memorial stone, and the organ screen also, were erected by John Reade's brother Edward in 1860 after he had become master of Ipsden House.

The memorial stone to John Thurlow Reade at Ipsden, Oxfordshire.

It may seem a strange place to site a memorial to a well-loved brother, but the story behind it is even stranger. After John had left Rugby School he sought service abroad with the East India Company and in 1817 he left on his first journey to India. He was always devoted to his family and regularly wrote home to his mother. She, for her part, was in the habit of walking down the hill to the Wallingford road when a letter from John was expected, so that she could collect it personally from the carrier.

After a particularly long period without a letter Mrs Reade began to get rather worried, but some instinct told her on a certain day to walk down to the Wallingford road for news of her son. This she did and as she approached the site of the memorial stone she saw an apparition of her son in a state of distress. This convinced her that he was dead and buried without Christian rites. She persuaded the vicar to hold a burial service in church to give her son peace.

Later the East India Company informed her of her son's death in the area of Sehaarunpore and that his servants had buried him where he had died. This must be one of the very few occasions when a memorial stone has been erected on the place where a ghost has been sighted.

The wraiths of Watton

Three miles to the south of Driffield, East Riding of Yorkshire, on the A164 road to Beverley, the village of **Watton** lies at a minor crossroads. Before the Dissolution in 1539, there was a priory here, a double house for nuns and resident canons. The house known today as The Priory was probably the prior's house and is all that remains of the monastic buildings. It is one of the most attractive old houses in the area and it has seen many adaptations and changes. Although it now presents a Tudor style, much of the stonework is said to have been part of an eighth-century nunnery as well as of the medieval priory.

This tranquil old house and its environs are troubled by the wraiths of two women. Their stories are separated by centuries, but the roots of their heart-rending torments are similar.

The earlier spectre's story begins in Saxon times. During a time of peace following a number of Viking raids to kill, steal cattle and destroy buildings, the ancient nunnery had been rebuilt and rededicated to the work of God by Lord Fitzjohn of Knaresborough. Soon after the ceremony Henry Murdac, Archbishop of York, revisited the nunnery, and with him he brought a four-year-old girl whose bright eyes and blonde curls made her most attractive. It was not clear why little Elfrida had been brought here by Murdac, but his lofty position ensured that no questions would be asked and that his wish that the girl be reared in the name of Christ would be obeyed.

The attractive child grew into a beautiful young woman well aware of the effect her beauty had on the male residents of the village of Watton outside the walls of the nunnery. She was a flirt and, despite the efforts of the Mother Superior and the other nuns, she was impossible to contain and control. The inevitable happened, and she became pregnant by a local lad who wanted then to wed Elfrida. The Mother Superior would hear nothing of it and, fearing for her own status and position when Archbishop Murdac got to hear of the matter, she was unduly harsh in the punishment of Elfrida. The young pregnant woman was locked in the deepest, dankest dungeon, fed only on bread and water and chastised daily for her sins. Some of the novices who had to minister to the reckless Elfrida feared that she would not live through the term of her pregnancy, but she did. She gave birth to a surprisingly sturdy baby boy, who was immediately removed from the tortured beauty, never to be returned. Soon after the birth, perhaps through complications or maybe through sheer exhaustion and a broken heart, Elfrida died in her cold cell.

Her death was not complete, however, for she is still seen, dressed in her nun's habit, roaming the land north of the present church in an area defined by grassy hillocks. She utters heart-rending wails for her lost child and perhaps his long-dead father.

The Priory itself is the focus of the second Watton wraith. During the Civil War she was the lady of this Royalist household. At the time of her demise she and her two young sons were alone in the great house. Her husband had departed some time before, at the head of village retainers, to place himself under the command of the king.

It was early afternoon and a scouting party of Parliamentarian troops had ridden out from Beverley, outside which their main force was camped. Their intention was to assess the enemy strength prior to a march north to Driffield, but when they saw that the potential Royalist stronghold at Watton was apparently deserted the small troop decided that there could be some sport.

The Roundheads battered down the door, taking only long enough to allow the lady and her sons to seek refuge in a previously prepared 'secret sanctuary'. (The exit from this hideaway led out to the garden and possible safety.) On this occasion the family stayed put partly because the troop's horses were tethered close to the exit and partly because the soldiers had found their way to the wine and beer cellars and had given up any thought of anything else.

Having drunk their fill but still just sober enough to realise that their mission was not yet completed, the Roundheads roused themselves from the cellars and returned outside the house to mount their horses.

It was at this moment that one of their number noticed the exit of the escape route behind the shrubs. He drew his sword and, followed by others, he brushed aside the shrubs and passed into the darkness of a short tunnel. When he emerged it was into candle-light and the presence of mother and children. The younger boy screamed and, for his pains, had his skull smashed in by the hilt of the trooper's heavy sword.

The elder boy leapt to protect his mother but was no match for his battle-trained assailant and was run through by the same sword which had caused the death of his brother. The frightened, hysterical, defenceless mother was then slain by the sweeping arc of the sword which severed her head. The whole episode took only seconds, and then regret and remorse at the rashness of the actions became paramount. The other members of the troop took prisoner the perpetrator of the dastardly act and, after a summary court martial, he was hanged. The three victims were given a Christian burial, but this has certainly not appeased the Royalist mother for, headless, she still walks the corridors, rooms and grounds of the old prior's house.

A house divided

Two miles north-west of the town of **Hawes** at the head of Wensleydale in North Yorkshire, on the north side of the A684, is Rigg House. The house is situated close to the lovely Cotter Force, one of the many idyllic becks and waterfalls of the Dales, and overlooks the young river Ure, which threads its sparkling way the length of Wensleydale and beyond.

No longer is this tranquil place troubled by the spectre of a headless woman. Reputed to have been a former housekeeper in the residence, she was employed by a surly, much disliked man by the name of Metcalfe. He had returned, very rich from money made partly in the slave trade, to the dale of his birth to live out his life in this most peaceful retreat. Unfortunately he was not well received, perhaps owing to jealousy of his riches but also because of his connections with slavery, as is borne out by the nickname he was given, 'Black Whipper'. His unpopularity did not help his humour and it would seem that he took out all his frustrations and anger on his only 'friend', his housekeeper.

She disappeared suddenly and mysteriously and this did not help to improve Metcalfe's popularity, for it was not long before 'behind-the-hand' accusations and gossip were being put about linking her disappearance directly to the hand of the Whipper. Things became intolerable for Metcalfe and without warning or preparation he vanished from the area.

The mystery did not end, however, for shortly afterwards Rigg House became haunted by what has always been considered as the housekeeper's spectre. It would seem that the manifestations took place only in one part of the property. Could it have been that

Rigg House and Rigg Cottage, Wensleydale, North Yorkshire, showing the haunted section demolished.

location where the murder took place? In any event the hauntings did not stop until that section of the building was physically removed. In practical terms this then left two houses – Rigg House and Rigg Cottage – but no ghost: a drastic but very effective exorcism!

The uninhabitable house

Eight miles east of Winchester along A272 is the village of Hinton Marsh in Hampshire. Less than a mile further along the road is a turning to the right leading to **Hinton Ampner**, the church and the manor-house being on the right.

For a number of years a very frightening set of ghosts haunted the old manor-house, the site of which is some 50 yards from the present manor, to such an extent that eventually it had to be demolished as no one was prepared to share it with the ghosts. Nevertheless the spirits were so strong that they were, to a lesser degree, to disturb the owners of the new dwelling from the period it was built in Georgian times until it was largely burnt out in 1960. No ghostly phenomena have been reported since the second re-building.

It is very difficult trying to piece together a story which could adequately explain the hauntings, as they were rather nebulous and indefinable. A memorial plaque in the church bears the name of one of the principal personalities in the affair, Honoria Stewkeley. She came to Hinton Ampner House after her sister Mary had married Edward Stawell in 1719.

After Mary died in 1740 rumour had it that there was an affair between Honoria and Lord Stawell, as Edward was then, and much gossip concerning them was spread by the servants in the village. This included a report that a baby was born to Honoria and was murdered in the hope that any scandal could, in this cruel way, be avoided. Honoria died in 1754 and Lord Stawell lived for only one more year.

For the following ten years Hinton Ampner House was little used, but in 1765 a family by the name of Ricketts rented the house and took up residence there. William Ricketts, the husband, was a wealthy merchant who spent much of his time travelling, leaving his well-educated wife Mary alone with their servants. The servants as well as the mistress suffered from the ghostly activities, and they were not locals with a knowledge of the house's early history but were brought from London by the Ricketts.

The new household hardly had time to settle in before the disturbances began: the slamming of doors, the rustling of silk, the appearance of a tall lady dressed in dark clothes, the sound of music in empty rooms, heavy footsteps and a curious murmuring sound for which no one could account.

By 1771 yet another disturbance was added to the others. This took the form of an argument which invariably ended with bangs, crashes and piercing screams.

By the end of 1771 Mary Ricketts was so terrified of living in the place that she left, taking her children with her. This was not the act of a hysterical woman, for the decision was reached with the help of her brother and his friend. They had sat up night after night in the house and experienced the sounds of gunshots, groans and door slammings. After the Ricketts had left, the house was briefly inhabited by a family called Lawrence, but they left suddenly after only a very short stay.

About 1800 the house, much decayed, was demolished. During the demolition a skull, possibly that of a child, was discovered beneath the floorboards in the house.

The doctor who disappeared

Halfway down the High Street in **Conwy**, North Wales, is the Elizabethan house known as Plas Mawr. It is now the headquarters of the Royal Cambrian Academy of Art.

This story begins at the end of the sixteenth century with a series of very sad and unfortunate events centred on the watch-tower and the lantern room, which are linked by a very steep stone spiral staircase.

The master of the house had been away at the wars for over six months but his return was expected, and his pregnant wife and their three-year-old child were looking out for him from the windows in the watch-tower. As the evening wore on and there was no sign of him they began the descent of the spiral staircase. In the gathering gloom the mother, with her child in her arms, slipped on the smooth stone and fell down the staircase. The noise of their fall, followed by the cries of the mother and child, brought the housekeeper to their aid. Both were injured and so the housekeeper had them taken to the nearest available room, the lantern room. She then instructed a servant to bring the doctor as quickly as possible.

The old family doctor was not at home when the call came and so his young assistant, Dr Dick, attended to the patients as best he could. He remained with them until he realised that they were getting worse and that the mother was likely to give birth prematurely to her baby. At this the young doctor wanted to go and seek the experience of his senior, but the housekeeper would not allow him to leave his patients and locked him in the lantern room. She then sent a servant to bring the old doctor to the house with all speed. However, the servant was taken by a press gang and put on board ship before he could deliver his message. The housekeeper became very worried about her mistress, for no sound could be heard from within the lantern room and she received no replies to her calls. As she was about to unlock the door and enter, she heard the heavy tread of her master coming into the house.

Naturally he insisted on knowing where his wife and child were and the housekeeper quickly outlined the events to him. As soon as he had heard this he burst into the lantern room, only to find his wife, child and new-born baby all dead. Of Dr Dick there was no sign. Overcome with grief, the master slammed shut the door and locked it saying that he would not leave until Dick had been found to explain the whole affair.

For hour after hour he paced the length of the room, and his cries of anguish could be heard. Finally it is thought that he worked himself up into such a tortured state that he too fell dead at the foot of his wife's bed, where he was found the next morning.

Of Dr Dick no trace has ever been found, and the only assumption which can be made is that the terrified doctor tried to escape from the room after the death of his patients knowing that although he was innocent he would be blamed. The only possible exit was up the chimney which linked with others and also with passages. Up he went, driven and confused by fear, until he lost his way or was overcome by fumes and smoke from the house's fires. He never emerged, but sounds emanating from the chimneys ever since seem to indicate that his spirit is crying out in the hope that his remains will be found and given a Christian burial. The master, too, can be heard pacing the floor of the lantern room and crying out for his beloved wife and children.

Lewtrenchard church, Devon, in the village haunted by the White Lady.

A bride and four bridesmaids

North of Tavistock, Devon, near the A30, is the village of
Lewtrenchard, which is haunted by Susanna Gould, the White
Lady. She is dressed in white for she died on her wedding day, 19th
March 1792.

At **Great Melton**, south of the B1108 west of Norwich, one may
observe a re-enaction of a very sad evening. Four bridesmaids
were returning from a wedding to their houses at dead of night in a
coach pulled by four horses. Somewhere along the route a terrible
accident occurred, and horses, coach and bridesmaids vanished,
only to return in spectral form – the bridesmaids sometimes headless in their coach. When seen like this then there is trouble ahead
for the observer.

At **Meopham** in Kent, south of Gravesend on the A227, lived Dick
Bennett. He went to fight in the war against Napoleon. When he
returned, his wartime girlfriend from France followed him. This
naturally upset Dick's wife and she led the pair a merry dance. The
French girl became so disturbed by events that after dressing in her
finest orange gown she hanged herself. Now she haunts Steel's
Lane in the village.

Another marital mix-up is considered by some to be the back-
ground of another suicide. The lady in question on this occasion is
a Sarah Fletcher whose death on 7th June 1799, albeit by her own
hand, was adjudged by the jury at her inquest to be due to the

lunatic condition of her mind. This verdict allowed her family to give her a Christian burial and her tombstone can be seen on the floor of Dorchester Abbey Church, between Abingdon and Wallingford, Oxfordshire.

The inquest and the jury's findings were described as follows in *Jackson's Oxford Journal* of 15th June 1799:

'The lady put an end to her existence by hanging herself with her pocket-handkerchief, which she fastened to a piece of small cord, and affixed it to the curtain rod of the bedroom in which she usually slept. After a full investigation of the previous conduct of the deceased, and the derangement of her mind appearing very evident, as well as from many other circumstances, the jury, without hesitation, found a verdict – Lunacy. The husband of this unfortunate lady is an officer in the Navy and is now on his passage to the Indies.'

Only 29 when she died, Sarah was spoken of as a beautiful and charming person, well-liked in the Thames-side village of **Clifton Hampden**, where she lived a quiet and lonely life. She was neglected, unduly so some would have said, by her husband, a naval captain. If it was not a lack of beauty and charm that dissatisfied her errant husband, it may have been a lack of money, for the truth behind Sarah's 'lunacy' and ultimate suicide was the

The memorial stone of Sarah Fletcher in Dorchester Abbey, Oxfordshire.

fact that the philandering captain had gone so far as to arrange a bigamous marriage with a very rich heiress who lived far from his Clifton Hampden home. The luckless Sarah, however, heard of the affair and, just in time, was able to present her case as the ceremony was about to take place. Distraught and distressed, she returned directly home and committed the suicidal deed to end her sadness, or so she believed.

Her physical remains may be at peace in Dorchester Abbey Church but her spirit is not. She is still regularly heard and seen around her old home, now called Courtiers House, a gaunt redbrick Georgian mansion, to be found at the end of Watery Lane, which runs to the right of the Plough Inn. Some observers record her as bearing 'absolute grief' or 'tragic intensity' in her eyes, but there have also been reports of her smiling. She is recognised by her long black silk cloak and the purple-red silk ribbon woven into her curly auburn hair.

The last two lines on her tombstone make the following appeal:

May her Soul meet that Peace in
Heaven which this Earth denied her.

When will she aspire to this heavenly state, and what needs to be done to help her?

The delightful village of **Amberley**, West Sussex, lies north of Arundel up a turning off the B2139. The thatched cottages are dominated by the walls of Amberley Castle at the west end of the village. Nearby are the church and the haunted vicarage. The ghosts here are of a woman and child. Sometimes the child alone has been observed playing in the garden. During rebuilding at the beginning of the twentieth century the skeletons of a woman and child were discovered at the bottom of a shallow grave under the dining room. The bones were thought to be about one hundred years old.

4
ILL-STARRED LOVERS

The secret of the barricaded cupboard

A mile south of Junction 13 of the M1 where it leaves Bedford-shire for Buckinghamshire is the village of **Aspley Guise**. Here a house called Woodfield, in Woodcock Lane, is said to be haunted, but whether this haunting is fact or was invented for convenience is a matter of conjecture. Nevertheless the story is a fascinating one and contains many ingredients expected of a good ghost story – romance, anger, murder and blackmail.

The hauntings originated in the eighteenth century when the site in Woodcock Lane contained a house which was inhabited by a father and daughter. The strict father did not allow his daughter to associate with the local lads but when the father was away on business the daughter made up for lost time with the boys. On one occasion, however, the father returned earlier than was expected and through the windows of his house caught sight of his daughter and her boyfriend. The couple, unaware that they had already been observed, rushed to hide when they heard footsteps on the path. They hid in what was probably the only place large enough for them both, a large cupboard.

The father quickly realised where they were hiding and such was his fury that he immediately wedged the door of the cupboard tight shut and pushed heavy furniture against it. There he left the two to their miserable deaths.

Sometime later the ubiquitous Dick Turpin arrived on the scene. He broke into the house intent on larceny. The barricaded cupboard immediately drew his attention and on investigation he found the bodies of the lovers. Realising that some terrible story must be associated with his discovery, he roused the master of the house and at pistol point extracted the facts of the case. Using this information Dick blackmailed the father into offering him sanctuary in the house whenever he needed it, and so the two of them took the bodies from the cupboard and buried them under the floor of the cellar.

The lovers have not lain easily in their resting place for they are still reputed to haunt the house that now stands over their graves, while Dick, astride Black Bess, is the phantom horseman of the grounds around the house. On the strength of these hauntings a

The Old Swan Tavern, Woughton-on-the-Green, Buckinghamshire.

recent owner of Woodfield twice attempted unsuccessfully to claim a reduction on his rates.

Four miles west of this haunting is the village of **Woughton-on-the-Green**, now in the environs of the new city of Milton Keynes in Buckinghamshire. Again evidence is found of Dick Turpin and his refusal to rest peacefully.

Attention is focused on the picturesque Old Swan Tavern, which in Turpin's time contained a windowless cell-like room in the centre of the building. This was called the prison room and served as a custodial place for prisoners in transit. Turpin, however, always on the lookout for safe houses, especially between his two favourite roads, the Watling Street (the A5) and the Great North Road (the A1), used the room for his own purposes, while the inn was a useful source of gossip concerning who and what was travelling the roads of the area. So fond of this area and secure here was Dick in his heyday that he can still be observed journeying between the two roads, especially along Bury Lane to the east of the village. If he is caught sight of, the hoof prints, if any, left by Bess should be checked, for it was in this area that Dick reversed her shoes to confuse the constabulary while making good his escape!

The soldier and the nun

That area of **Brighton** known as 'The Lanes' is all that remains of the small ancient coastal town of Brighthelmstone. Nowadays it is one of the attractions of Brighton, drawing visitors who wander round the crowded narrow streets, one of which is called Meeting House Lane. While strolling down this, you will come across a bookshop, opposite which is a bricked-up doorway in a wall. This doorway was blocked in the nineteenth century but it is still used by the ghost of a nun.

Beyond this wall, in the twelfth century, was the priory of St Bartholomew, and during the nun's lifetime it was being guarded by soldiers. The nun fell deeply in love with one of the soldiers and her love was reciprocated.

They decided to elope and make a life together. Unfortunately their absence was soon noticed and a party of soldiers was sent out after them. They were captured and brought back to the priory. The soldier was executed for desertion and the nun was walled up in a tiny space and left to die of starvation. This was the traditional way of disposing of nuns who had broken their vows as it entailed no blood spilling by the senior members of the order. While the miserable nun was dying her slow death, psalms and prayers for her spirit were said in the chapel. Evidently not enough was done to satisfy this particular nun's spirit, for it is still abroad today!

The actress's lover

Drury Lane Theatre in London has a ghost which the actors and management are always pleased to welcome because the only time he manifests himself, or so it seems, is when the theatre is about to put on a successful, long-running production. Another

Meeting House Lane, Brighton, East Sussex, is haunted by a nun.

Drury Lane Theatre, London, where the 'man in grey' presages a long-running production.

strange thing about him is that he has never been seen at night. Matinee audiences have seen him and so have many of the theatre workers during the morning.

One theory put forward concerning the 'man in grey', and supported to some extent by evidence discovered during the re-building of the theatre, states that the man was of noble birth and lived in about the 1770s. He was a well-known figure in the theatre at that time and a frequent visitor, probably because he had a lover amongst the actresses. This actress, it seems, may have had a jealous suitor who picked a quarrel with her noble admirer and cruelly stabbed him to death. The body was then hurriedly bundled into a short, little-used service passage to the left of the stage, and there it was bricked up.

However, in the rebuilding in the nineteenth century, the service passage was opened up and there, a crumpled heap on the floor, lay the skeleton of a man with a short dagger still in place through his ribs. Upon the skeleton were the vestiges of his clothing, made of a grey material!

The wronged maiden of Ringstead

The skeleton found in a ditch near a particular orchard in the village of **Ringstead** in Northamptonshire, six miles north of Rushden, had no such cloth remnants to provide clues concerning the ownership of the bones, but other information was apparent and this indicated that they were the mortal remains of a young woman of the village who had disappeared fifteen years before in 1850. The length of the bones showed the corpse to be of the same height as the missing girl, and the skull had the same two teeth missing that the villagers remembered Lydia Attley had been lacking. All those years earlier, before she went missing, stories had linked her in love with a local landowner and butcher by the name of Weekley Ball.

The relationship formed between the two was not very stable and Ball soon tired of the girl, but Lydia was not to be cast aside, especially when she became convinced she was carrying Ball's child.

She soon realised that she was not going to regain and hold his love, so she began to threaten to expose him and demand money. An assignation was made to meet in Ball's orchard one night to settle the matter. The meeting did take place since a passing labourer, returning home late from work, overheard through the boundary hedge Lydia exclaiming with a voice full of anxiety, 'You plan to be rid of me tonight, Weekley Ball.' Without stopping, enquiring or intervening, the labourer continued homewards, not telling his story for another fifteen years.

Not until the discovery of her skeleton in the ditch which ran alongside Ball's orchard – their final meeting place – were attempts made to piece together the full story of Lydia's disappearance. Weekley was arrested and charged with murder but, when brought to trial, he had to be acquitted because the evidence against him was uncorroborated and far too flimsy to convict and hang him.

His neighbours in the village and the surrounding area, uncontrolled by the niceties of the law, remained convinced of his guilt and treated Ball accordingly. Ultimately he was obliged to sell up and leave the district.

Throughout this fifteen-year period and beyond Lydia was not at rest or at peace. Her silent nightly vigil varied between walking from the orchard to the place in the ditch where her remains were discovered, and walking towards the church but only as far as the gate. At this point she pauses and looks about her, before turning on her heels and returning to the orchard, where her apparition fades and disappears.

The joke that turned to tragedy

Apart from the busy road running through the village, **West Wycombe**, Buckinghamshire, with its coaching inns and seventeenth- and eighteenth-century houses, is a pleasant place to visit. Our story is centred on the fourteenth-century George and Dragon inn with its ghost of a White Lady. She was Susan, a servant at the inn, and a great beauty. Although the locals tried to court her she held herself aloof, hoping for a finer catch. There was a fine, well-dressed young man from the city who frequently stayed at the inn on his travels. Susan served him well and he seemed to show some interest in her.

The locals were somewhat aggrieved at the way things were developing and so they decided to have some fun at Susan's expense. Immediately after the fine visitor's last stay at the inn, three of the lads sent Susan a note purporting to come from her admirer. The note instructed her to obtain a bridal gown and to meet him at the entrance to the caves, which are situated halfway up the hill on which the church stands. From there they were to go and be married. When evening came and Susan had completed her duties at the inn, she changed into her newly acquired gown and slipped secretly away from the village up the slope to the caves.

There she was confronted by the three locals, who made no effort to disguise their merriment at the situation they had created. Naturally enough Susan did not take kindly to this, and she retaliated by hurling stones at the three youths. In the ensuing struggle Susan fell heavily and fractured her skull on a rock. This quickly brought the three to their senses and they rushed Susan back to the inn. Alas, she died that night, and her unquiet spirit has haunted the room ever since. Her presence is heralded by a rapid fall in the temperature of the room and she is usually observed in the early hours, probably at a time coinciding with her death.

Murder in the church

Penfound Manor, Cornwall, which is not open to the public, claims to be the oldest inhabited manor in Britain. It was mentioned in the Domesday Book as belonging to Queen Edith, wife of Edward the Confessor, and part of the Saxon building can still be seen as also can the Norman, Elizabethan and Stuart additions. To reach it leave Bude on the A3073 to join the A39 after one mile. Turn right and drive four miles towards Poundstock. Turn left at the sign indicating that Penfound Manor is half a mile away.

The Penfound family has more than one ghost – if you visit the

The George and Dragon Inn, West Wycombe, Buckinghamshire, is haunted by a serving girl.

village of Poundstock with its refurbished Gildhouse set in the corner of the churchyard by the lychgate, you will look up to the serenely beautiful church dedicated to a most eminent Catholic saint named Winwaloe. We are not here to investigate him, but a member

Penfound Manor, Poundstock, Cornwall.

of the Penfound family (who have been lords of the manor for centuries), William Penfound, who, in 1357, was assistant curate to the rector. Mass was just finishing on 27th December, the Feast of St John the Evangelist, when uproar arose in the church. It transpired that local rogues and robbers, of whom, it must be said, William was one, had quarrelled. The period at the end of Mass had been chosen as a time of reckoning. It was not a pleasant episode, and at the end of it William was dead – stabbed and clubbed countless times, with blood and entrails strewn and splattered in many parts of the church, including the altar. The upshot was that the bishop excommunicated the perpetrators and they were hunted down and locked away in Launceston Castle. Poor William may have been dead, but still he has no peace or time for reflection, for he seems doomed to pace the holy place where his life was so violently curtailed.

Each 26 April it is said that the other Penfound ghosts can be seen. They re-enact a seventeenth-century scuffle at Penfound Manor, when Nicholas Penfound tried to stop his daughter Kate eloping with John Trebarfoot – all three were found dead.

The rejected churchwarden

Among the by-roads north of Berkhamsted, Hertfordshire, to the right off the B4506, is the village of **Little Gaddesden**. Its Elizabethan manor-house was, in the eighteenth century, the home of a churchwarden named William Jarman. He committed suicide because the love he had for a local lady was not returned. Some say he hanged himself in the house, others that he drowned in the village pond. The latter is more likely for it is the pond which he now haunts.

North-east of York lies the attractive village of **Sheriff Hutton**. It can be reached by turning left off the A64 from York. In the coaching era there lived in the village Nance and Tom. Tom was a coachman who worked on long runs to the extreme north of England and Nance was his girlfriend. During one of his absences Nance fell for the charms of a gentleman from London and ran away with him. Tom did not see her again until one dark night he spotted a bundle of rags beside the road as he was driving his coach towards York on what is now the A64. It was Nance, who with her baby, had been left destitute by her lover, and she was on the point of death when found. Soon Nance and her child died and Tom's sorrow was great, but he had not seen the last of Nance. She would often appear to him when he was driving his coach through adverse conditions to guide him safely on his way. She still supplies this very commendable service to present-day travellers along the main A64.

A beautiful Spanish noblewoman might seem out of place in a remote part of rural Lincolnshire, but that is where you may encounter Leonora Oriedo – or rather, her ghost. In 1596 a British force captured Cadiz and Leonora fell in love with Sir John Bolles, who led the British force. Bolles did not tell her that he was already married, and when he had to leave Leonora begged to accompany him. She was so persistent, offering him all her fortune, that he had to tell her that he was married. As Sir John sailed out of the harbour Leonora killed herself, but her ghost followed him and now frequents the area round his home, **Thorpe Hall**, near Louth.

The jealous sister

Berry Pomeroy has a medieval castle, which has within its walls a roofless mansion of late Tudor or Jacobean times. Both castle and mansion have their ghost stories. To get there, leave Totnes on the A385 driving east. After almost a mile leave the main road and take the route signposted to Berry Pomeroy village straight ahead. Continue through the village and take the left fork beyond. On reaching the castle lodge gates (where tickets should be bought) on the left, proceed down the half-mile drive to the castle itself.

From the Norman Conquest until 1548 the castle belonged to the family of de la Pomerai, and for some time during this period its mistress was Lady Eleanor de Pomeroy. She had a sister, Margaret, living there at the same time and, as fate would have it, they fell in love with the same man. Eleanor seems to have been less successful than her sister in winning this man's attentions for she became very jealous of Margaret. Such was her position that she was able to win the man's affections for herself, but only by having Margaret imprisoned in the castle dungeons and kept at starvation point, and here she remained for a long time until released by death.

The tower, which can be seen at the extreme right-hand end of the wall leading from the gatehouse, is Margaret's Tower and the dungeon can still be visited. It is from here that Margaret now rises in spectral form, displaying all her former beauty. She makes her way up to the castle ramparts and endeavours to encourage persons who see her to join her. The legend is that after the appearance someone will die.

Inside the medieval castle walls is a large open space forming a courtyard for the Tudor mansion. This is a tall three-storeyed building which, probably towards the end of the seventeenth century, was left in the care of a steward for many years. The best authenticated sighting of the ghost of the mansion occurred during this time.

A local doctor from Torquay, Walter Farquhar, was called to the mansion to attend the steward's wife. He was asked to wait in a lofty oak-panelled room with a staircase in one corner. As he gazed around at this fine apartment a beautiful woman entered in a very distressed condition. She paid no attention to the doctor but ascended the staircase, disappearing from view at the top. The doctor was somewhat puzzled by this but said nothing on this occasion. He attended the steward's wife and left saying he would return soon to see what progress had been made.

At the time of the second visit the patient was much improved and out of any danger. The doctor reported this to the steward and then went on to remark about the distressed young woman he had

The gatehouse of Berry Pomeroy Castle, Devon, where Margaret Pomeroy was starved to death.

seen on his first visit. On hearing the story the steward became very upset and explained to the doctor that she was an omen of death. The last time she had been seen was when the steward's son was drowned. The doctor assured him there was nothing to worry about – his wife was well on the way to regaining her full health. But later that day the steward's wife died!

5
GHOSTS FAR AND WIDE

The most haunted area of England

Borley, Essex, is said to be the most haunted area of England. To get there go north on the A134 from Sudbury, Suffolk, for two miles to Rodbridge Corner. Turn left and cross the river Stour and then a disused level-crossing. Immediately beyond these turn left for Borley church, less than a mile away, on the right-hand side.

The churchyard itself contains some interesting topiary work, but a less permanent feature is the ghostly figure of a nun which has frequently been observed moving along the path to the church or passing from tree to tree. Her other haunt was across the road at Borley Rectory, which was burnt down in 1939.

While in the churchyard you may hear footfalls and yet see no one, or you may hear organ music coming from within the church, but on entering find that there is nobody seated at the organ. These are but two of the ghostly phenomena which may assail your senses in this remarkable place.

Many books have been written about the activities of the ghosts of Borley Rectory and this section will merely whet the ghost hunter's appetite. The nun mentioned earlier is possibly the oldest ghost here. Borley Rectory was built on the site of a monastery and seven miles away at Bures there was a nunnery. In the thirteenth century living at the nunnery was a novice who had fallen deeply in love with one of the Borley monks. They decided to elope, but inevitably were caught and punished. The novice, in accordance with practice, was walled up alive in a small niche and allowed to die of asphyxiation or starvation, whichever came sooner.

A more plausible story, however, was revealed during seances held at the rectory. The spirit voice heard was that of Marie Lairre, a nun who came to Borley from Le Havre in the seventeenth century. Later she married Henry Waldegrave, who lived in a house on the site of Borley Rectory. But they were unsuited to each other and on 17th May 1667 Henry strangled Marie and buried her beneath the cellar floor. Harry Price, the celebrated psychical researcher of Borley, led a group who excavated beneath the cellar floor and unearthed the remains of a young woman. The remains were given a Christian burial at Liston churchyard in 1945.

During the tenancy of the Reverend and Mrs Foyster from 1930

Borley church, Essex, is the subject of many ghost stories.

to 1935, the busiest period in the ghostly history of Borley, messages were seen to materialise on walls and on pieces of paper demanding 'light', 'mass' and 'prayers' – all things missing from the original interment and death of the nun from Le Havre.

Strange smells, voices, coaches and horses, other ghostly figures, missiles thrown around, bells rung – they have all happened at Borley! Its end came at midnight on 17th February 1939 when the rectory caught fire and was gutted. Even this had been foretold during a seance in December 1938. The destruction of Borley Rectory has not, however, brought an end to the activities of its ghosts and fresh sightings are regularly reported.

The leper in the Bird Cage

The broad thoroughfare through the centre of the old market town of **Thame** in Oxfordshire is interrupted by a group of buildings which splits the area, forming on one side the Buttermarket and on the other the High Street.

The most prominent and interesting building in this central

group is the inn called the Bird Cage, an unusual name derived, it is thought, from the former use of the building as the town lock-up. The building originally dates from the thirteenth century, when it may have been used as a retreat for lepers who were tended by monks and nuns. It is the spirit of one of these unfortunate lepers who haunts the upper part of the building by knocking loudly on one of the ancient walls. No ghost has been seen but during seances contact with a troubled spirit was made. This spirit did not like being called up: it was very unhappy, hated people and had no faith in God, and it certainly did not want exorcising. From this it would seem that the leper's knocking was deliberate in that it signified no plea for help but was done solely to irritate, annoy or frighten the Bird Cage's human inhabitants.

During renovation work at the Bird Cage the 'knocking wall' was stripped of its original internal facing and a large gaping hole was revealed which exuded an unaccountably pungent odour, but no physical remains could be discovered.

The Thame area is rich in ghosts, for in addition to the leper at the Bird Cage and the murdered farmer there is the Grey Lady of Rycote, who has been frequently seen at **Rycote Chapel**, a few miles west of Thame.

The Bird Cage, Thame, Oxfordshire, was haunted by a leper.

Rycote Chapel, Oxfordshire.

The numerous ghosts of Pluckley

Drive south-east from Maidstone on the A20 to Charing and turn right on to the B2077 for the drive of about three miles to **Pluckley**, Kent. This is the 'safest' way into the village for just about every other road into and around it is the haunt of at least one ghost.

Park by the Black Horse on the left and cross the road to the lane opposite, but take care, for a phantom coach and horses charge down this village road. Take a stroll down Dicky Buss's Lane. Keep your eyes raised to the branches of the trees and you may see the body of a man swinging by a rope from his neck. This is the ghost of the village schoolmaster who hanged himself from a tree along the lane.

The church of St Nicholas is the resting place of a couple of Lady Derings. One, known as the Red Lady, wanders the churchyard in search of a baby which she lost. The second Lady Dering was considered a great beauty. When she died her husband encased her in four coffins, three of lead and an outer one of oak, in order to preserve her beauty from decay. She was dressed for the burial in her best gown with a red rose at her bosom. All these elaborate preparations have not succeeded in confining her to her resting place for she too is on ghostly duty in the church. A third Lady Dering, the White Lady, still haunts the burnt-out ruin of her former home, Surrenden Dering, a mile to the east of the village.

Having turned the corner past the church, walk down to the junction on the left where Greystones stands, and you may meet the ghost of a long dead monk; or continue on to Rose Court and listen out for the ghost of the old lady who calls in her dogs. Further down this road, near the station are the old brickworks with their deep clay pits, into one of which a man fell to his death. Since then his ghost has re-enacted the scene complete with an ear-piercing scream.

Returning towards the village, take the turn on the left which passes by Park Wood, where the figure of a soldier, a colonel no less, still enjoys his ghostly walk along the public footpath.

At the junction with the B2077 turn right and then left along a lane which leads down to the stream and the little stone bridge. By the water's edge the ghostly figure of a gypsy woman, a watercress seller, has been seen puffing contentedly at her pipe. Her end was a sad one, for during her rest period she dozed off and the pipe, falling from her mouth, set fire to her clothes and she burned to death.

Close by are the remains of a hollow oak which once served as a hiding place for a highwayman. It was his practice to leap out on unsuspecting travellers and rob them. Unfortunately for him it became his death-place when a wary traveller pierced the oak with his sword, thus impaling him. The highwayman has 'died' innumerable times at this place during soundless re-enactments of this disastrous episode.

The haunted village of Prestbury

Little separates the village of **Prestbury** from the town of Cheltenham these days, but at the time of the Domesday Book of 1086 this area north-east of the larger settlement had only 36 inhabitants and was owned by the Bishop of Hereford. However, Prestbury retains a definite village atmosphere, and this will be confirmed during the following walk.

Park the car in the free area indicated first left then right past the King's Arms and the war memorial. From the car park walk across to the right to join Mill Street and head down the sloping street towards the church. It is along this street that the first Prestbury

ghost may be met, or rather sensed, perhaps not by human aware-
ness but more probably by the dog if it has been brought along for
the walk. For generations past local farmers, drovers, coachmen
and more recently pet walkers have had problems encouraging
their animals along the lane between the church and the Plough
Inn. No one can account for it but hackles rise, horses rear, dogs
growl and cower, while cats hiss and avoid the area. (When
passing either of the two gates to the churchyard on the left, while
proceeding down Mill Street, one may notice the back of a hooded,
black-cloaked figure but his story will be told later.)

The area around the crossroads at the foot of Mill Street is
probably the oldest part of the village. To the left is the Burgage: in
the middle of the thirteenth century the right was granted to hold a
three-day fair here in August, as well as a weekly market.

The village walk continues across into Lake Street, which was
once the site of a lake belonging to the monks of Llanthony Priory,
who stocked it with fish. At the end of this cul-de-sac there is a stile
to the right of the three-storey house called Shemara. The field
path curves round to the right and beyond there is a fine view of
Cheltenham Racecourse. The half-mile field walk re-enters the
village in Park Lane, which is of little interest until the crossroads
with Shaw Green Road and Bowbridge Lane are reached. In the
unlikely chance that the walk is taking place at dawn in the spring

The Plough Inn, Prestbury, Gloucestershire.

or autumn, listen for the sound of a galloping horse's hooves. A glance in the direction of the sound will reveal a Cavalier in full flight for Gloucester, fleeing from the battle of Worcester. His flight is brought to an abrupt end as he is hit in the chest by an arrow, which completely pierces his breastplate, killing him instantly.

Curiously this same manifestation has also been reported beyond Bowbridge Lane where it becomes the Burgage, ending opposite Prestbury House. Here the story goes that the residents of the house were anti-Royalists and had set a booby trap for unwitting Cavaliers abroad at dead of night. The trap consisted of a tight rope spanning the village street at the height of a horseman's neck or head. The horseman heard on these nights is a Cavalier who was carrying messages for the King's commanders but who rode into the trap and was garrotted: another abrupt end!

Both of the two versions may be true, but evidence for the arrow-shot death is stronger, for in 1901, during roadworks in Shaw Green Lane, workmen unearthed the skeleton of a man with an arrowhead still firmly embedded in his chest.

Further south along the Burgage, on the right is Sundial Cottage, which takes its name from the dial set high on the southern gable end. Also on the gable end is carved the date 1672.

While examining these two features one may hear the melodic

Prestbury House, The Burgage, Prestbury, Gloucestershire.

strains of a spinet being beautifully played: this is the cultured lady ghost of Sundial Cottage engaged in her most delightful haunting. She may be heard both in the house, where she has also been seen on the landing, and on summer evenings in the garden.

At the end of the Burgage is a T junction and the way to the left is Tatchley Lane. On the opposite side of the road there used to be a range of courtyards and stables serving the large nineteenth-century houses facing on to Prestbury Road. The stables no longer house horses but have been converted into very desirable modern residences. Names such as Mews and Coachman's Cottage recall the origin of the properties, but the one of paranormal interest is Walnut Cottage, named after the tree to the right of its entrance. In its heyday it was the coach-house and its most famous resident in those days was Old Moses. This is known because on more than one occasion when he has popped in for a visit and has been asked by the tenant of the time who he is the response has been, 'I be Old Moses just in to see thee.'

This is a very pleasant response considering the manner of his murderous demise in the attic room of the coach-house, perpetrated by person or persons unknown, not to mention the major changes which have subsequently altered his haunting place.

From Tatchley Lane turn left at the five-ways crossroads into Deep Street. The first house on the left, a large and imposing establishment, is known as The Three Queens but bears no name-plate. It is so named because it was built and extended during the years 1547 to 1603, when three queens, Jane (the Lady Jane Grey), Mary and Elizabeth, ruled the nation.

An intriguing question is raised by the large empty niche dominating the front façade above the main portico. Just who or what once occupied it remains a mystery but perhaps there is a connection with one of the two ghosts reputed to haunt this venerable building.

The older of the two manifestations is that of a black abbot who moves silently about the house causing starts and surprises to present-day inhabitants, but no other problems. The second presence also has ecclesiastical connections, for he is a former vicar of the parish who still potters about in the hall and the study where, when not preparing a sermon that is never to be preached, he is quite happy to have a chat with all comers.

Further up Deep Street, Reform Cottage could easily be missed, for it sits well back from the road, almost hidden behind an old terrace of three stone houses dated 1550. These are reputed to have been the infirmary belonging to the monastery of Llanthony, and beside the door on the house nearest Reform Cottage a scribed circle in the stone is thought to be a dial to tell the monks when it was time for mass. The land adjacent to the old infirmary and in front of Reform Cottage is considered by some to have been the burial ground for the monks. Was this a reflection on the success rate, or lack of it, of the infirmary?

At this point it is necessary to reintroduce the hooded figure seen first of all near the church. He may now be seen approaching Reform Cottage across the monks' burial ground. Observe carefully and he will be seen to pause at the front door of this sixteenth-century partly weatherboarded former tithe barn before knocking and entering. Later, sounds of movement in the attic, footsteps and items being displaced and falling to the floor can be heard but when these upper rooms are inspected nothing is ever found to be out of place or broken.

The prime occasions on which to observe these hauntings appear to be on the eves of Christmas, Easter and All Saints. There is also an oral tradition of an underground passageway linking Reform Cottage and the church.

Leave Deep Street and bear right along High Street, where the dominant building is the King's Arms. As the most important hostelry in the village for the past three hundred years, it must have many a tale to tell, but none of them seems to be of ghosts and spectres.

On returning to the corner by the war memorial and almost back to the car, one will find a house on the left called Cleeve Corner. This private residence was once a lodging place for the monks of Llanthony Priory but following the Dissolution it became a farm-house. One of the house's bedrooms was the scene of a horrific murder, an event which can be exactly replicated on any night. There are two versions of the story but the basic facts are the same: in one version a young and beautiful bride was strangled by a thief who broke in and stole her wedding gifts and jewellery; in the second version the strangler and thief was her newly-wed husband. Whoever caused her death was never caught and still disturbs the environment within the house by piercing lights, chill draughts and a clammy atmosphere. This is not all for, if the murder room is inadvertently used for some unwitting guest, the strangler is more than ready to repeat his evil murder, unless the victim can voice a prayer while he or she still has the breath left to do so.

Ghosts of the Essex coast

Leave Chelmsford in an easterly direction on the A414 passing through Great Baddow, Danbury and Runsell Green. Approximately three-quarters of a mile from the last village leave the main road and follow the B1010 towards Purleigh and Cold Norton. From here the road goes on through Latchingdon and Snoreham

The Chapel of St Peter, Bradwell-on-Sea, Essex, is sometimes lit by ghostly light.

and on to Asheldham; then follow the B1021 to Tillingham and eventually to **Bradwell-on-Sea**. On approaching the church turn right past the mounting-block outside the church gate and the village lock-up. Drive along this village lane until Eastlands Farm is reached. Park on the left and continue on foot along the gravel track for about half a mile. This track was once the line of the Roman road leading to the fort of *Othona*. It is little wonder that one of the ghosts of the area is thought to be a Roman horseman, whose horse is heard, but never seen, galloping either along this track or across the country on your left from a farm called Weymarks to the site of the fort. (If you want the opportunity of actually seeing a Roman legionary then you should visit **Mersea Island**, across the Blackwater estuary to the north, where many sightings have been recorded.)

At the end of the track the chapel of St Peter ad Murum is reached. This fascinating chapel is one of the oldest in Britain, having been built in 654 by St Cedd from materials taken from the older Roman fort. Furthermore it is thought to be on the site of the gatehouse of the fort and this partly accounts for its solid condition in that it is sitting squarely on firm Roman foundations and not relying for support on the shifting sand of the area. The chapel has had a somewhat chequered history. It was reconsecrated as late as

1920; prior to that it was in use as a beacon tower in Elizabethan times, a watch-tower during the time of the Stuarts, a smugglers' lair in Georgian times, a grain store when Victoria was queen and subsequently as a cattle shed.

On occasions, even in recent years, a light has shone out from the chapel and yet on investigation no source from which this light could emanate has been discovered within. However, ghostly shapes might be seen moving slowly about, not clear enough in form to identify, and making no sound.

Leaving the chapel and walking over the sea wall a hundred yards to the south, you will find the 200-year-old coastguard house, now the headquarters of a birdwatching society whose hides can be seen along the shore near the house. For over a hundred years this was the home of the Linnet family. Walter, the last member of the family to live there, died in 1958. It seems, though, that he still keeps a watchful eye on his old, well-loved home, for since his death a ghostly figure answering his description has been seen peering in through the windows, observing the present part-time tenants. To obtain a closer look, he has at times wafted in through the window to materialise within the room. Unfortunately it is only his upper half which can be seen. Perhaps he is still a novice as ghosts go and he has not yet learned how to materialise the whole of himself!

The photogenic ghosts

Leave Wincanton in a south-westerly direction on the A303 to Sparkford; then take the A359 to Marston Magna. Turn left at the signpost to Rimpton and continue on this road towards **Sandford Orcas**, Dorset. One of the first buildings reached in the village is the church, which is said to be haunted by the jangling of keys and the pitter-patter of running feet.

Beside the church is a short drive leading into the courtyard of Sandford Orcas Manor. The car may be parked here before entering the manor grounds. Take your camera with you when visiting this haunted house for the ghosts of Sandford Orcas are very photogenic. The owner has a series of photographs sent by visitors to the manor, which show unexplained figures on the prints!

One of the ghosts, noted for her prompt appearance, is a lady who can be met on the spiral staircase at 11.50 a.m. each day. Even if you do not see her, that cold draught which you feel is yet another way in which she manifests herself.

A little dog, which has recently been photographed but which died about 1900, may be seen. You may also observe a man in armour, a man wearing a ruff, or an evil-looking man dressed in evening clothes. No one seems to be able to provide stories to link in with these ghosts but they are there and they do appear.

There is, however, one ghost to whom we can attach a story, and that is the tenant farmer who now haunts the manor, often by peering in through the kitchen window between 2.30 p.m. and 3.55 p.m.. He was found dead in the house after having hanged himself many years ago.

Sandford Orcas Manor is well worth a visit. It is not a 'set piece', but a genuine lived-in Tudor manor with all the atmosphere of a home.

Ghostly duellists and a phantom ape

North-east of Dorchester, Dorset, along the A35, just over a mile beyond Puddletown, **Athelhampton Hall** will be seen on the left beside the main road.

The hall dates from early Tudor times and for much of its existence it has been the home of the Martyns, a Catholic family. Like Sandford Orcas it has many ghosts, ranging from black priests to grey ladies, including a ghostly cooper who hammers away at non-existent wine casks and barrels in the cellar.

An interesting story is told of the Great Hall, where once a woman guest was sitting alone reading. Suddenly the door was flung open and two young phantom swordsmen came duelling into the room. They disturbed the woman and she asked them to take their troubles elsewhere. They took no notice of her complaints

Athelhampton Hall, Dorset, is haunted by an ape.

until one was wounded in the arm. At this they turned on their heels and disappeared back through the door.

A very unusual ghost haunts the hall in the form of an ape. The Martyns' family crest features an ape, and they kept apes as pets. The manner in which this particular ape came to haunt the hall is rather sad. The story is that a daughter of the house had been jilted in love and in her frustration she rushed from the library through a secret door, used as a priest-hole, up a hidden staircase and into an upper room, slamming shut the second secret door. She was not aware that one of the pet apes had followed her from downstairs and was sealed in by her closing the upper door. There it remained and lingered on until it died of starvation. After death its spirit continued to haunt the secret staircase for years afterwards. The girl is reported to have committed suicide, but probably more as a consequence of the lost lover than of the death of the ape.

The haunted bedroom

Creslow Manor in Buckinghamshire is situated to the north-east of Whitchurch off the A413 Winslow road and has an interesting history dating back to the reign of Edward the Confessor. The manor-house itself has undergone many alterations over the centuries and the portion of the house which is haunted consists of a crypt, probably dating from the earliest times, and a chamber above with a Gothic doorway and windows.

The best authenticated series of events associated with its female ghost, Rosamund Clifford, occurred around the middle of the nineteenth century when the owners of the manor were holding a dinner party at their residence. When the party ended there was a heavy storm blowing. The guests were offered accommodation for the night and all accepted, but this meant that all the rooms would have to be used. The room over the crypt, although made up as a bedroom, was never used because of the hauntings. One man, however, was willing to risk a disturbed night as long as he was allowed to make certain preparations. The owners agreed and so he armed himself with a cutlass, a brace of pistols, some candles and a box of matches. He then retired to the room.

When he was alone he checked the room thoroughly and securely locked both doors. With matches and candles beside him he slipped into bed and was soon asleep. A few minutes after midnight he was roused by the rustling of silk. Quickly he lit a candle but there was nothing in the room which could have produced such a noise. He settled back in his bed and went to sleep again. It was not long before he was more rudely awakened, but this time the rustlings were such that they indicated a struggle. The man jumped to his feet and moved in the direction of the noises with arms outstretched so as to let nothing pass him. But he touched nothing and the rustling faded away. He returned to bed again and lit a candle, which this time he left burning while he slept fitfully through the rest of the night.

The king's standard-bearer

Claydon House, Buckinghamshire, can be reached from Creslow Manor by returning to Whitchurch, turning right and driving through pleasant countryside and the villages of North Marston, Botolph Claydon and Middle Claydon. Claydon House lies half a mile to the south of the last village.

The Verney family purchased the estate in 1471 and the family still lives there though the sixteenth-century house has been added to and altered over the years.

Although it is the haunt of a number of ghosts, the most interesting of them is that of Sir Edmund Verney. This very gallant gentleman had the honour of being the king's standard-bearer at the battle of Edgehill in 1642. When Cromwell's men overran the standard and Sir Edmund was captured, he was told to surrender the colours, but he refused, saying: 'My life is my own but my standard is the king's.' At this he was killed, but his slayers found it impossible to take the standard from the dead man's grasp; they were therefore forced to sever his hand from his body in order to

Claydon House, Buckinghamshire.

carry off the colours. The standard was later recaptured by the king's forces, still held tightly in the death clasp of Sir Edmund. The hand could be identified for it wore his signet ring. No one knows where or even if Sir Edmund's body was buried, but after the battle the hand was removed and returned to the Verney family to be interred.

Although the ghost has not manifested itself recently, on numerous occasions it has been recorded that Sir Edmund Verney, minus his right hand, has been seen around his old home, apparently searching for the place where it was interred.

Civil War skull

Both sets of protagonists in the 'Commonwealth Commotions' have their fair share of ghostly lingerings. This is not to be unexpected, for the energy and fervour generated in many people at all stations and levels of English life must have left a strong residual spirit power not easily soothed regardless of the final outcome of the Civil War.

In this story it is one of Cromwell's supporters who, if specific requests are not adhered to, finds it difficult to remain at peace in **Chilton Cantelo** church, Somerset. Wounded during the conflict, Theophilus Brome was a Warwickshire man who rapidly left his home county at the cessation of the Civil War troubles for fear of retribution from his local opponents. He travelled south and settled in Royalist country in his sister's home at Higher Farm, across the lane from the church, in Chilton Cantelo. It was here that he lived out his life, always remaining true to his past beliefs, and he made sure that all his friends and family were quite clear about his wishes come the time of his death. Like his neighbours, he requested a Christian burial for his body, but for his head he wanted something different.

He died on 18th August 1670 and his body was buried, but only after his head had been removed. This was kept in its own special box in a cupboard above a door in the hall of the farmhouse and it is still there, it is reported. The key to it was lodged in the bank for total security. The reason for this odd request was the practice, at the time of the Restoration, for Royalists to open up the graves of supporters of the Commonwealth and remove their heads to be displayed in public places in order to deter any renewed upsurge in anti-Royalist activities.

Evidence to confirm these facts came to light in 1864-5, when the church was being restored. For some reason it was decided to open up the Brome tomb and, sure enough, there was the body but not the head. Fortunately the body was reinterred and restored to its resting place within the sanctity of the church. Today the memorial capping stone can be found on the north side of the church, behind the pew next to the organ, hard against the wall. This is a very dark spot and the seventeenth-century text is worn in places but it states:

> Here lyeth the body of
> Theophilus Brome of the
> Bromes of the house of
> Woodcowes neere Warrwick
> Towne in the county of
> Warrwick who deceased 18th day
> of August 1670 being 69
> Yeares of age just
> in the actions of his
> life true to his freinds
> Forgave those that wronged
> him & dyed in peace.

The ghostly activity displayed by Theophilus, as is usual in these cases, manifests itself only when persons not of the spirit world think they know best and want to 'do the right thing' by attempting to reunite his body and skull, or simply to inter the skull in the earth. This activity is not popular with Theophilus and he responds with frightful and horrid noises which soon dispel the do-gooder's enthusiasm.

The solitary mourner

Lyme Park is a National Trust property maintained by the Metropolitan Borough of Stockport. It is about five miles south of Stockport, to the right off the A6, about half a mile before the village of Disley. The park surrounding the hall covers more than 1300 acres of moorland and parkland and is a delightful recreational area with lakes and deer amongst the trees.

Lyme Hall has been the home of the Leghs since 1346 and the

Lyme Park, Disley, Cheshire.

early members of the family were great soldiers. The property was granted to the Leghs by the king for the bravery shown by Sir Piers in rescuing the Black Prince's standard at Caen. His son, another Sir Piers Legh, succeeded his father in 1399 and followed him by fighting for the king in France. He was with Henry V at Agincourt and later died from wounds received in battle at Meux in 1422.

It had been his wish that his body be brought back to Lyme Park for interment. Long after his burial the funeral procession became one of the ghostly activities of the park. This is hard to understand for Sir Piers was brought home for burial as he had asked. The drive is a long winding one through the park beside the lake, and seeing this solemn and ghostly procession making its slow, steady way to the hall must have been rather awe-inspiring.

In more recent times the vision has been limited to what is thought to be a solitary mourner, the rest of the cortège having ceased to manifest itself. This lonely apparition is a woman, head bowed in sorrow and grief, but strangely dressed in a white head-dress and gown.

Not knowing her true identity, the people who have observed this ritual have named the woman Blanche, and legend has it that she was the secret mistress of Sir Piers Legh. Not having been able to attend the actual burial of her lover, she is doomed to act out this charade for the rest of time. Great must have been their love and greater her sorrow at his death.

Some audible ghosts

In the village of **Willington**, east of Bedford, the Georgian manor is said to be haunted by the heavy footfalls of a man and a tinkling bell. During rebuilding in the early twentieth century the skeleton of a man was found bricked up in a wall.

Around **Spinney Abbey**, in Cambridgeshire, on dark nights you

Willington Manor, Bedfordshire.

can watch mysterious lights gleaming and listen to the sweet singing of long dead monks. Connoisseurs of ghostly singing should also visit the village of **Zennor**, near St Ives, Cornwall,

The effigy of a mermaid in the church at Zennor, Cornwall.

which is approached from a turning off the B3306. In the church is the effigy of a mermaid who caused the death of a local chorister. This young man unwittingly lured the mermaid from the sea by his wonderful singing. She in turn tried to return to her watery home with the chorister but he was drowned, and now his ghostly singing is heard when wind and weather make the sea rough and dangerous.

North-west of Poole off the A350 lies the village of **Lytchett Matravers** with its haunted Whispering Corner, which forms part of the Church Path. At any time of day or night if you pause at this corner you may hear the chatterings and mutterings of a group of phantoms. Unfortunately it is not possible to distinguish the words and we therefore have no clue as to what they are discussing so urgently.

The Priory at **Burford**, Oxfordshire, between the B4425 and the river Windrush, can boast a number of ghosts ranging from a small monk dressed in brown to a bell which unaccountably rings at 2 a.m. The nearby rectory houses a poltergeist – an unhappy malevolent spirit, which hurls articles about and causes a terrible noise.

Ghostly animals

In the Vale of Glamorgan **St Donat's Castle**, west of Barry off the B4265 towards the coast, was haunted by a series of unusual ghostly phenomena. Strangest of all was the phantom panther which paced the corridors. There were bright lights in the bedrooms, like staring eyes, a witch in the armoury and a piano which could give out pleasant music without human assistance and even

Burford Priory, Oxfordshire.

Salisbury Cathedral, Wiltshire, where phantom birds circle the spire.

with the lid shut!

Transparent white phantom birds wheeling round the spire of **Salisbury Cathedral** are harbingers of death for one of the clergy associated with the cathedral, so states a firmly believed local story.

Up in the Chiltern Hills to the east of Wendover, Buckinghamshire, is the village of **Cholesbury** with its iron age fort and, on moonless nights, one can hear the terrifying sounds of grunts, snaps and snuffles from small phantom pig-like creatures who fight among themselves in a most vicious way.

Sheringham and **Cromer** in Norfolk are connected by a coastal footpath. If the night is dark and the wind is howling then you may see Black Shuck, the phantom dog of Norfolk. The closer you are to the coast the greater is your chance of observing this terrifying creature. Another canine ghost of East Anglia is even more terrifying and dangerous to behold. This is a huge black hound with bright gleaming eyes whose home is the Devil's Ditch west of **Newmarket**. To see this creature means death or insanity in a very short time.

Towards the head of the majestic and dramatic dale of the river Swale in North Yorkshire, on the B6270, a mile and a half east of the village of **Muker**, is a narrow lane leading off to the north. After passing through a copse the lane crosses the Swale by means of one of the most elegant ancient stone bridges in England, Ivelet Bridge. With its sweeping arch, it is narrow and steep and not ideal for modern motor vehicles for, although the bridge is still in use, its original purpose has long since passed into history. But the visitation by a headless black dog does not allow the memory to fade. This bridge was built in part to carry the Corpse Way across the river, since it was not thought seemly to risk fording the Swale in

Devil's Ditch, Newmarket, Suffolk, is the haunt of a ghostly hound.

At Ivelet Bridge, Swaledale in North Yorkshire, a headless hound is a portent of death.

spate whilst carrying a coffin containing the body of a relation or friend to burial in consecrated ground. All the settlements from Keld at the head of the dale used the Corpse Way to bring their dead to Grinton church twelve miles away. This custom continued until 1580, when a chapel of rest was erected at Muker. The way is still open and is regularly walked by locals and visitors. The stones and barns known as Dead Houses, resting places for the coffins along the way, can still be seen, as sometimes can the headless Ivelet Hound, a portent of death,who is observed slipping silently up the arch of the bridge to the top, where he equally silently disappears over the parapet.

Phantom horses and spectral coaches

To the south of **Hungerford** in Berkshire the A338 is kept busy with ghosts by day and night. During the day be prepared for a galloping white horse with a lady rider to cross your path and fade from view on the other side of the road. At night the road resounds with the rumbles and clatters of a coach and four at full speed. While driving along the lanes through the beautiful country around **Charlbury** on the B4022, north of Witney, Oxfordshire, do not become too interested in the sights around you. Keep a watch out for a huge white stallion which leaps hedges and charges riderless across your path.

It is perhaps not surprising that ghostly horses should be met in the Berkshire Downs, for there the elegant shape of the **Uffington**

The White Horse at Uffington, Oxfordshire, is re-shod by Wayland every hundred years.

White Horse, now in Oxfordshire, has graced the hillside since time immemorial. Nearby is Wayland's Smithy, a neolithic long barrow, and legend has it that any horse left at the smithy, with payment, will be found mysteriously shod when the horse's owner returns. It is said that once a century the White Horse of Uffington leaves its hillside to be shod at Wayland's Smithy, and the last time this happened was about 1920. Some men were drinking one night at an inn below the hill, when a man entered. He was dressed in old-fashioned clothes, with a leather apron and a tall hat and sat alone with his drink. Suddenly the sound of a horn pierced the night. As it was repeated the newcomer rushed out, and then came the noise of galloping hooves, as if from the sky. The drinkers ran outside; the sound was now very loud and directly overhead. Then they noticed that the White Horse had disappeared from the hillside. The galloping seemed to head in the direction of Wayland's Smithy, and a little later the horse was seen back in its position on the hill. Those present believed that the visitor to the pub was Wayland himself, and that he was summoned by the White Horse for his centennial re-shoeing.

Not far from Uffington is the **Letcombe Brook** near Wantage, Oxfordshire. Here, when grave national danger is imminent, one may hear the sound of hundreds of horses crossing the stream. The water made turbulent by their hooves can be seen, but the beasts themselves are invisible. This phenomenon was reported just before the Boer War, and again before the First World War.

One of the former owners of **Wolfeton House**, Dorset, two miles north-west of Dorchester, a member of the Trenchard family, won a wager by driving a coach and horses up the great staircase. He must have been very proud of this feat for his ghost repeats the act. Another of the Trenchards, a woman, committed suicide by cutting her throat and now haunts the house headless and dressed in grey.

The Trenchards are not alone in driving a coach and four through their home, for they were possibly preceded by Sir George Blount of Kinlet in Shropshire. He was a significant landowner in the attractive Wyre Forest area of the county. His sixteenth-century seat was at the tiny village of **Kinlet**, which lies to the north-west of Bewdley at the junction of the B4194 and the B4363. If the unsignposted lane opposite the former B road is taken then in a short distance the remotely sited parish church will be seen on rising ground ahead.

This well-kept and delightful-looking double cruciform church was built by the Blounts beside the family's manor-house. To reach the church, even today, worshippers must go through the cutting under the footbridge, past the mounting block, used when horses were the main means of transport, through the kissing gate and along the church path.

Inside the church in the north-east corner there is a monument depicting Sir George, his wife and his two children, John and Dorothy. Evidently their problems started when Dorothy, whom Sir George idolised, went against his express wishes and eloped and married a page-boy or some other servant employed in his household. This action was certainly not what he had in mind for

Kinlet church, Shropshire.

the future of his favourite child and only daughter. Being an obstinate and irascible man throughout his life, Sir George swore vengeance for the rest of time on Dorothy and her new family, so when he died in 1581 the haunting was inevitable.

A favourite manifestation of the ghostly squire was for him to rise up out of a local lake shouting and urging on the four plumed white horses drawing his coach. His shouts, together with the pounding of the hooves, the snorting and panting of the horses, and the rumbling of the coach's iron-shod wheels on the coarse stone driveway, made this a horrific sight under a moonlit but cloud-scattered sky. When, however, the family experienced this while they were at dinner in the hall, and the coach and four with Sir George at the reins hurtled in through the double doors to rampage the length of the table, the situation became not only frightening but intolerable.

The result was inevitable. In 1720 the original manor-house was abandoned and razed to the ground after a new residence had been built further from the church and at a higher elevation. This house remains and is now a boarding school, untroubled by the ghost of Sir George.

A group of the clergy are said to have met to exorcise the ghost. This took place in the church, focusing on the monument. The turbulent spirit is reputed to have been lured into a glass phial and securely stoppered, so ending the disturbances. It is not clear, however, what happened to this unusual bottle of spirit. Some say it was cast into the sea, but others say it was left in the church. Do

Hughenden Manor, High Wycombe, Buckinghamshire, haunted by Disraeli.

take care if on a visit a discovery is made!

On Dartmoor, around **Tavistock**, Devon, Sir Francis Drake may sometimes be seen and heard riding with his phantom hounds. On other occasions he has been seen near the A386 Tavistock to Plymouth road in his black coach drawn by four headless horses. Another great man who seems reluctant to leave the area he loved is Benjamin Disraeli. His ghost has often been observed on the upper floors of **Hughenden Manor**, his home two miles north of High Wycombe, Buckinghamshire.

Ghosts of soldiers… and Nell Gwynne

North-west of Peterborough, Cambridgeshire, is a sparsely populated area which, during the Civil War, saw a number of minor skirmishes. Involved in many of these was Michael Hudson, who led a band of Royalists in harassing the Parliamentary troops. Eventually the band was cornered in **Woodcroft Manor**, between the villages of Werrington and Helpston. They would not surrender but fought through the house from room to room until only Hudson remained on the roof and still fighting. Eventually he was beaten back and he slipped, only just managing to hang on to the parapet by his fingertips. On seeing this, one of his enemies rushed forward and hacked off his fingers! Hudson fell screaming to the moat below and death. His voice is still heard calling for mercy from his murderers.

The ghost of another Cavalier haunts **Salisbury Hall**, now the Mosquito Aircraft Museum, a mile south-east of London Colney, Hertfordshire, and close to Junction 22 of the M25. He was ambushed by Roundheads and shot himself when he realised that escape was hopeless. Charles II had the place fitted out as a country retreat to which he could escape from London with Nell Gwynne. The lovely Nell must have enjoyed life at Salisbury Hall for her ghost, dressed in blue, still frequents the place.

A more recent ghost haunts the area near the tomb of the Unknown Warrior in **Westminster Abbey**. He is a sad-faced, khaki-clad soldier of the First World War period.

Beeleigh Abbey, a mile west of Maldon in Essex, was the home of Sir John Gates, until he was beheaded on Tower Hill on 20th August 1553 because he had supported the cause of Lady Jane Grey. His ghost, dressed in military uniform, paces smartly about the abbey with his head held in the traditional ghostly place, underneath his arm.

A miscellany of ghosts

The ghosts of **Woburn Abbey**, Bedfordshire, the seat of the Duke of Bedford, surprisingly have not been turned into money-

Woburn Abbey, Bedfordshire.

spinners by the Duke, who has been forced to commercialise his heritage. But then they are very limited and unpredictable in their activities. They mysteriously open locked doors, even when the locks have been changed, and produce cold, clammy sensations on the faces of onlookers.

North of Bedford are the villages of **Ravensden** and **Wilden**. They lie to the east of the B660 and are linked by a twisting lane which is haunted by the ghost of a witch dressed in black and with an evil grimace on her face. She does no harm but promptly disappears as viewer and ghost draw level.

Chenies Manor House, near the A404 east of Amersham, Buckinghamshire, has a fascinating history including connections with Henry VIII, Anne Boleyn, Charles I and a lame priest whose limping footsteps were heard before the occupants of the house discovered a priest's hole in the Pink Room. On the wall of this secret place was the date 9th September and a year in the 1660s. On the anniversary of this date ghostly phenomena are expected in the house.

The Royal Hotel at **Hoylake**, Merseyside, has a mysterious ghost inasmuch as there appears to be no reason for his haunting. In himself there is little that is mysterious; in fact he is quite ordinary, dressed in tweeds and cap and wandering the corridors. **Capesthorne Hall** in Cheshire, on the A34 north of Congleton, houses a number of ghosts. A group of shadowy figures descends to the family vault, a lady in grey floats along the ground-floor passages, and, most interesting of all, a severed arm reaches out towards and rattles an upstairs window!

From the village of **St Levan** near Land's End, Cornwall, a ghost ship in full sail has been seen heading straight for the coast. On reaching the shore it does not stop but sails over land to fade from sight outside the village of Porthcurno.

Two miles north of **Widecombe-in-the-Moor**, Devon, on the

B3344 lies the grave of Mary Jay, who hanged herself in a barn which once stood on this site. The legless figure of a man swathed in a dark blanket has been seen crouching at the head of the grave, and perhaps it is he who places the fresh flowers which so mysteriously appear from time to time on the grave.

At **Ilford**, Essex, the old fire station in Broadway is said to house the ghost of an old fireman in full fire-fighting regalia. He is thought to be Godfrey Netherwood, who served there during the 1890s. Some say that he has moved with the brigade to the new station in Romford Road.

Another unusual ghost requires careful driving in Cambridge Gardens, **North Kensington**; for there is a phantom double-decker bus which, although solid-looking, vaporises to nothing on reaching the St Mark's Road junction.

Winchester Cathedral attracts many visitors each year and some, armed with cameras, may well be surprised when they receive their exposed film back from processing. Several people have obtained photographic evidence of ghostly monks walking in procession through the cathedral. Usually the monks are seen walking on a level below that of the present floor, for during the passage of time the cathedral floor has been raised.

Abthorpe, three miles north-west of Silverstone in Northamptonshire, has a ruined manor-house, in which two ghosts are confined. One, a Franciscan friar, roams the house and grounds, thus indicating that sometime in its long history the house must

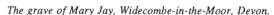

The grave of Mary Jay, Widecombe-in-the-Moor, Devon.

The Kenton Theatre, Henley-on-Thames, Oxfordshire.

have had religious connections. The second ghost is female and dates from the seventeenth century. She is said to be Jane Leeson, who, when she died, granted money for the founding of a school in the village.

A female figure, thought to be May Blandy, who was hanged at Oxford in 1752, has haunted two places in **Henley-on-Thames**, Oxfordshire, when a play about her was being produced. The haunted places were the town hall and the Kenton Theatre. Not only was she seen but also she caused lights to be switched on and mirrors and other articles to be smashed.

Thorington Hall, Suffolk, east of Nayland on B1068, above the river Stour, is a gabled farmhouse of the sixteenth century. The ghost of a girl dressed in a simple brown dress tied at the waist with a cord wanders the dark upstairs passages.

The A2270 north of Eastbourne, East Sussex, near **Willingdon**, was in Edwardian times the scene of a motoring accident when two

Highworth church, Wiltshire, where a priest haunts the churchyard.

men and a woman lost their lives. The men seem content with their lot, but the woman has become known as the Grey Lady of Willingdon, and she can be seen beside the road waving her arms as if attempting to slow the traffic to a safer speed.

North of Swindon, Wiltshire, on the A361 is the village of **Highworth**, where the churchyard is haunted by a priest. The earliest reports stated that this ghost was observed in daylight in bright sunshine. In those days he was dressed in a long dark cloak. Recent sightings have reported him dressed in white, flitting from window to window of the church, peering in but never entering. Those who have been close to him have observed that he has no face, just a grey mass with two darker blobs for eyes.

The Lady in White haunts the area around **Avebury Manor** in Wiltshire. Dressed in white lace with a white hood, she is a pleasant sight to behold. She has been known to take walkers by the shoulders and turn them away from a field gate for no apparent reason. The manor itself is haunted by rose petals which are found strewn across the floor of the Crimson Room. The doors and windows are opened by some ghostly hand even when checks have been made to secure them.

Avebury Manor, Wiltshire, is haunted by rose petals and its neighbourhood by the Lady in White.

6
ROYAL GHOSTS AND ROYAL PALACES

William Rufus, the wailing queen and the Black Prince

The old **Cadnam** to **Romsey** road in the New Forest, Hampshire, is reputed to be haunted by the ghost of William Rufus (William II) who was killed while hunting in the forest on 2nd August 1100. When his body was discovered it was taken by cart to Winchester, and it is along this route that Rufus may be seen on the anniversary of his death.

The village of **Castle Rising** lies north-east of Kings Lynn, Norfolk, on A149. The castle was once the home of Isabella of France, consort of Edward II. She was a depressed and sometimes violent woman, and it is these aspects of her character which the inhabitants of the area are forced to remember. Her ghostly screams and wails are still to be heard within the castle ruins.

When travelling along the A2 between **Bexley** and **Dartford** in Kent do not be amazed if you are confronted by a man in armour. It is only the ghost of the Black Prince who used to stay at Hall Place in Bexley.

The king's nurse

One of the commoners haunting the palace of **Hampton Court**, Middlesex, is Mrs Sybil Penn, nurse to Edward VI. She was still living at the palace in the reign of Queen

Castle Rising, Norfolk.

Elizabeth I and contracted smallpox at the same time as the queen in 1568. The queen recovered from her attack, but poor Sybil died on 6th November and her body was buried at St Mary's Church, Hampton. In 1829, during a severe storm, the church was struck by lightning, and a new church was later built.

Although Sybil Penn's tomb and effigy were removed to the new church her grave was violated and her remains were disturbed. It was possibly this occurrence which has caused her spirit to return and haunt her old home. She is a kindly old ghost who works diligently at her spinning-wheel, which is frequently heard near her old apartment, and, dressed in long grey garb, she walks amongst the visitors to the palace. Her spinning-wheel was found, after a search had been made following complaints about its noise, in a sealed room in the south-west wing.

Another part of Hampton Court, Fountain Court, was at one time haunted by two male figures who caused disturbances at night and these hauntings ceased only after workmen installing new drains discovered the bodies of two Cavaliers, perfectly preserved, beneath the courtyard surface. The bodies were given a Christian burial and Fountain Court enjoyed peaceful nights once again.

Anne Boleyn's headless drive

Anne Boleyn was the second of the ill-fated wives of Henry VIII and although she became the mother of a future queen of England, Elizabeth I, she could not give Henry the son he so dearly wanted. So Henry had her beheaded on 19th May 1536, when she was not

Blickling Hall, Norfolk.

Hever Castle, Kent.

yet thirty. Many of the happiest days of her life were spent at **Blickling Hall** in Norfolk, and though the present hall was not built until almost a century after her death she returns to haunt the area each year on the anniversary of her execution. In a wild drive round the countryside she rides in a coach pulled by headless horses and driven by a headless coachman. Anne also is headless; her head rests comfortably secure in her lap despite the rolling and lurching of her coach. The climax of the trip is the triumphal entry into the drive of Blickling Hall on the completion of this memorial ride. At the head of the drive the whole apparition gradually dematerialises, until another year has passed.

To reach Blickling drive north from Norwich along the A140 to Aylsham, then turn left along the B1354 for less than two miles to Blickling church. Immediately beyond, the straight drive and formal gardens of the hall come into view.

Anne Boleyn spent much of her childhood at **Hever Castle** in Kent and in the gardens was courted by Henry VIII. Her ghost is said to walk across the bridge over the river Eden at Hever each Christmas Eve.

Jane Seymour and Catherine Howard

Anne Boleyn's successor as Henry's queen was Jane Seymour, and her ghost is one of the many to be seen and heard in the Tudor palace of **Hampton Court**, Middlesex. She glides about the Clock Court, holding before her a lighted taper, and also wanders through the Silverstick Gallery and down the stairs.

Henry's fifth wife, Catherine Howard, is the noisiest and most disturbing of the ghosts of Hampton Court. When about to be taken into custody and accused of being unfaithful to her king, she, knowing what her end would be, in an effort to convince Henry of

The Clock Court at Hampton Court Palace, Middlesex, where Jane Seymour carries a lighted taper.

her innocence, rushed screaming through the palace to the chapel where he was at prayer, but all to no avail – Henry would not be disturbed; her captors caught up with her and dragged her off, still shrieking. On each anniversary of her short-lived escape, her spirit re-enacts the screaming race to the chapel along what has since been named the Haunted Gallery.

The grateful queen

Drive south out of Cambridge on the A10 for three miles to Trumpington. Turn left here on to the A1301 through Great Shelford to **Sawston** village. Turn left at the war memorial and a hundred yards along on the right is the entrance to the drive leading to Sawston Hall, built in 1584, and the home of the Catholic Huddleston family for over four hundred years. The hall contains the finest priest-hole in England, located in a turret in the centre courtyard.

The ghost of Sawston Hall is Mary Tudor and the story begins early in July 1553 immediately before her accession to the throne. Her brother, Edward VI, was dead but Mary was not aware of this when the powerful Duke of Northumberland asked her to come to London. During this journey she stayed at Sawston Hall. Northumberland hoped to take her prisoner there and then to place his daughter-in-law, Lady Jane Grey, on the throne.

Mary had retired to bed in the Tapestry Room on the night of 7th July when, in the early hours of the following morning, John Huddleston, master of the house, received warning that Northumberland's men were in the area searching for Mary. Quickly he roused the future queen and, disguising her as a milkmaid, helped her to escape before the traitors reached his home.

Before Mary was out of sight of Sawston Hall she must have seen and heard the terrible commotion made by Northumberland's men when they arrived at the hall and found that she was not there. In their fury they set fire to the Huddleston house. As Mary turned

Sawston Hall, Cambridgeshire, has a bedroom haunted by Mary Tudor.

on her horse and saw this, she is supposed to have remarked: 'Let it burn; when I am queen I will build Huddleston a finer house.'

She was as good as her word for by the year 1584 the present building was completed, using stone from Cambridge Castle. The Tapestry Room, complete with the four-poster bed in which she slept, which survived the fire, is the haunted room, though she has been seen in the grounds also. Her ghost is observed moving majestically, as one might expect, and never making contact with the living, unless the ghostly music which is sometimes heard emanating from a non-existent virginal is her method of communicating with us across the centuries.

George II and George IV

At **Kensington Palace**, London, pause awhile as you walk past and gaze along the windows, for in these windows has been seen the face of George II. This was one of his residences and he died here in 1760.

Brighton's famous Pavilion, built by the Prince Regent, later George IV, was sold, complete with ghosts, to the town during the reign of Victoria for £50,000. The Dome concert hall, in George's day, was the stable for the Pavilion, and linking the two were underground passages, along which the king's ghost has been seen walking. The other ghost of the Pavilion haunts the kitchens in the form of Martha Gunn, the famous bathing woman of Brighton. She often frequented this place during her lifetime.

Royal Pavilion, Brighton, East Sussex.

The ghosts of Windsor Castle and the Great Park

There have been many reports of ghostly phenomena in and around **Windsor Castle**. The cloisters near the Deanery are reputed to be the haunt of Henry VIII, who manifests himself with the sounds of ghostly groans and slow, dragging footsteps. Elizabeth I has been seen in the Royal Library on many occasions. She walks, tall and austere, without a sidelong glance, to disappear again from mortal eyes at the limit of the library area.

Windsor's most famous and well-authenticated ghost is that of a young guardsman who shot himself while on sentry duty on the Long Walk in 1927. A few weeks after the death of this guardsman, two soldiers met on the Long Walk. One had just completed his period of sentry duty and the second soldier, who was to relieve him, thought he seemed very eager to leave the area. The second soldier had an uneventful turn of duty – all had been quiet though the night was very dark. It was close to 2 a.m. and the soldier heard the steady tramp of marching feet – his relief was on its way. He decided to make one last patrol along the area under his control. He completed the outward length, turned smartly to return to his post, and as he began to march observed a guardsman marching towards him. As the figure came closer his eyes could make out greater detail in the darkness, until finally he saw the smiling face of the guardsman who had committed suicide at that spot!

As the true relief party came closer, however, the phantom faded and disappeared. The soldier was rather taken aback by this occurrence, but on his return to barracks he recalled how eager his friend had been to relinquish his post to him. He went to his friend's bedside and, after some careful questioning, the two soldiers realised that they had both been confronted by the ghost of their former comrade.

Herne the Hunter

A centuries-old ghost of the Long Walk, Windsor Great Park and the Forest is that of Herne the Hunter, who was a royal forester in the time of Richard II. During a hunt a stag, wounded by the hunters, in pain and desperation turned on its attackers and charged in the direction of the king. Seeing this, Herne threw himself on the neck of the stag to save his king. After a fierce struggle the stag was stabbed to death, leaving Herne badly mauled and close to death. As the king and huntsmen gathered round the gored body of Herne, it was apparent to all that no matter what they did Herne would die. Then a stranger appeared and told the king that he could save the brave hunter's life if Herne could be carried to the stranger's hut on **Bagshot Heath**, seven miles away to the south. The king agreed and urged the stranger to do all he could to save Herne. The foresters were instructed to make a bier for Herne, while the stranger cut off the stag's head and placed the antlers on Herne's head. As the party carrying the bier was departing, the king promised Herne that, on his recovery, he would be promoted to head forester, as a reward for his bravery.

On the journey to Bagshot Heath the foresters became more and more disgruntled at the king's last words to Herne, and when they reached the hut they tried to persuade the stranger not to care for Herne but rather to let him die. The stranger would not break his promise to the king but a compromise was worked out. It was arranged that Herne would live but he would not enjoy his promotion and the foresters would have to live with the blood curse of Herne upon them. This they agreed and the stranger prepared to make Herne well again.

When Herne recovered he returned to **Windsor Castle** and the king made him his chief forester. However, it was soon apparent to all that Herne had lost his skill as a forester and huntsman and therefore the king dispensed with his services. Herne could not live with the disgrace of his dismissal, so on that very night he went out into the forest and hanged himself from an oak tree.

Following Herne's death his fellow foresters began to realise the effect of his curse upon them; nothing went right for them in their service of the king. Things reached such a state that they returned to Herne's healer to try to find a solution to their problems. He told them that the ghost of Herne would have to be appeased before they would have peace.

Subsequently they gathered round the oak where Herne had hanged himself and called upon him. He appeared to them, complete with stag's antlers growing from his head, and instructed them that at midnight the following night they must assemble there with the king's horses and hounds.

This they did and for many a night afterwards the forest rang with the sound of the hunt. These hunts continued until not a deer was to be found in the forest. King Richard, after many a fruitless hunting trip, demanded to know what was wrong and the foresters told their story. The king then went to the oak and received the word of Herne that his deer would return if the foresters were punished for their part in the troubles. The king had the foresters put to death, the deer miraculously returned to the forest in abundance, and Herne was heard of no more during the reign of Richard II. But after the death of the king Herne resumed his activities, but now alone, and on occasions his horse's hoof-beats are heard and, more rarely, the sound of his horn.

Herne's Oak is said to have been destroyed in a violent storm in 1863.

An eighteenth-century engraving of Herne's Oak, Windsor Great Park, Berkshire, from which the brave hunter hanged himself when dismissed from his post as chief forester.

FURTHER READING

The British Isles are amazingly well endowed with the presence and evidence of ghosts of all descriptions. From time immemorial they have fascinated the populace, and for this reason almost every district, regional centre or tourist information department seems to produce a pamphlet or booklet on the subject.

For more detailed and sustained reading the following are recommended:

Archer, Jean. *Tales of Old Buckinghamshire*. Countryside Books, 1987.

Brooks, J. A. *Ghosts and Witches of the Cotswolds*. Jarrold Publishing, 1990.

Brooks, J. A. *Railway Ghosts*. Jarrold Publishing, 1985.

Cunniff, Tom. *The Supernatural in Yorkshire*. Dalesman Books, 1985.

Findler, Gerald. *Ghosts of the Lake Counties*. Dalesman Books, 1969.

Grey, Edward. *Ghost-hunters Guide to Britain*. Reader's Digest Association, 1985.

Hallam, Jack. *The Ghost Tour*. Wolfe Publishing, 1967.

Hole, Christina. *Haunted England*. B. T. Batsford, 1951.

Ireland, Kenneth. *True Ghost Stories*. Scholastic Publications, 1989.

McEwan, G. J. *Haunted Churches of England*. Robert Hale, 1989.

Mitchell, W. R. *Haunted Yorkshire*. Dalesman Books, 1969.

Underwood, Peter. *West Country Hauntings*. Bossiney Books, 1988.

Underwood, Peter. *A-Z of British Ghosts*. Chancellor Press, 1993.

Hauntings are among the strange, unexplained or curious events described in the Gothick Guides to counties published by Shire Publications. There are Gothick Guides to Cornwall, Devon, Hertfordshire, Norfolk and Northamptonshire.

Page numbers in italic refer to illustrations.